ROOSEVELT UNIVERSITY

From Vision to Reality

1945-2002

ROOSEVELT UNIVERSITY

From Vision to Reality

1945–2002

A TRIBUTE
by
THEODORE L. GROSS

ROOSEVELT UNIVERSITY
CHICAGO AND SCHAUMBURG

To My Roosevelt Family

Copyright © 2002 by Roosevelt University   Printed in U.S.A.   All Rights Reserved   ISBN Number 0-9632567-5-0

This brief account is a tribute to Roosevelt University, an institution I have been privileged to lead for the past fourteen years.

Born out of discrimination in the 1940's, committed to the inclusion of people of all racial and religious backgrounds, developed after World War II, the Korean and Vietnam conflicts, amidst an ever expanding metropolis, Roosevelt University has been a microcosm of Greater Chicago. The capital of the midwest finds its reflection in this private, nonsectarian, complex institution so deeply rooted in social justice and democratic values – it is indeed the academic child of Franklin and Eleanor Roosevelt.

I am grateful to those witnesses who were active during Roosevelt's birth and infancy and have lent me their memories: Rolf Weil, my predecessor as president; Frank Untermyer, professor of political science; and Jerome Stone, chairman of the board of trustees for many years. My own contemporaries – Vinton Thompson, provost; David Miller, professor of History; and Thomas Karow, assistant vice president of Public Relations – offered valuable commentaries on the text, especially in its description of the university during adolescence and maturity.

Beginning with several hundred students in 1945, Roosevelt has grown to 7,500 and become a comprehensive, metropolitan university with campuses in

Chicago and Schaumburg. It has transfigured itself into a new university for the twenty-first century, anchored by liberal arts and sciences and featuring professional colleges of performing arts, business, education, and adult learning. I can only hope that my tribute has done justice to those who laid the foundation and shaped the image of Roosevelt University, to the faculty and staff who cared for it during the past 57 years, and to the students who will perpetuate its legacy.

Tom Karow edited the volume and, together with graphic designer Ray Machura, organized the photographs that comprise our institutional memories and give life to my words.

THEODORE L. GROSS

President

May 1, 2002

Contents

2   Origins

52 Consolidation

90 A Metropolitan University

138 Commencement Speakers and Honorary Degree Recipients, June 1946 – April 2002

142 Index

ROOSEVELT UNIVERSITY

From Vision to Reality

1945-2002

Origins

EDWARD J. SPARLING

When Roosevelt University was created in 1945 it was considered an experiment in the imagination of Chicago. The city was segregated racially and religiously, and discrimination was prevalent in social clubs, corporations, housing – and in colleges and universities.

The Central YMCA College, which was the forerunner of Roosevelt, was no different from all those institutions that took discrimination for granted, and the Board of Directors sought to impose quotas on minorities. Edward J. Sparling, the first president, had been forced to deal with a YMCA rule barring African-American students from the swimming pool, and the best accommodation he could reach was that they would no longer be charged an athletic fee for facilities they were not allowed to use. One of the board members went even so far as to defend restrictive covenants as "the right of property owners to restrict their property against Jews, Negroes, children, dogs," and in November 1944, asked Sparling how many black students were enrolled.

He had asked the wrong man. Sparling's own ancestors had been expelled from Germany during the religious persecution of Protestants, and his lumberjack father had imbued him with the belief that "you can't blame a man for what he can't help being." He was a fearless idealist, Edward J. Sparling, and told the board that no such records were kept. The directors then asked Sparling to make a survey, which he agreed to do – so long, he told them, as the information was not used to establish quotas. An outspoken progressive who sometimes embarrassed the Board by speaking publicly in support of labor and against the suppression of minorities, he went further: he told the board he would resign if the survey were used to discriminate. The board then told him his "qualifications were not compatible with the requirements of the position of President," and suggested he quietly look for another job. On April 17, 1945, Sparling resigned under protest.

The faculty of the YMCA had been openly critical of what they considered to be its mismanagement,

1945 Central YMCA College, predecessor to Roosevelt College, provided higher educational opportunities for working people in Chicago at a time when most universities were not receptive to the education of part-time adult students.

1945 Roosevelt College was known as Thomas Jefferson College of Chicago for the first ten days of its existence. The name was changed when President Franklin Roosevelt died.

Although Franklin Roosevelt has been a wonderful namesake for the university, in the late 1940's, the founders of the college had a difficult time raising money from corporations because conservatives were hostile to many of Roosevelt's policies.

but there was little reform during the depressed academic world of the 1930's. The students who attended the YMCA College worked from midnight to dawn and then attended their classes. They were largely ignored by the administration. After Sparling resigned, the faculty cast a vote of 59 to 15 that expressed a lack of confidence in the board and then, by a vote of 62 to 1, decided that the college should break away from the control and direction of the YMCA. The students supported this decision by their own vote of 488 to 2.

Out of this crucible of racial and religious defiance was born an institution of higher learning committed to social justice. On April 2, 1945, even before his resignation, Sparling paid a $10 state fee for the articles of incorporation of Thomas Jefferson College, which was renamed Roosevelt College after Franklin Delano Roosevelt died on April 12, 1945. He installed an orange crate as his desk, and when he was told he might become president of an "all Negro, all Jewish" school, he did not blink: "If so I shall be proud," he answered "– so long as it's academically excellent."

The mass resignation by the president, faculty, and students was extraordinarily courageous since they had no alternative institution to go to, no student body in place, no building or equipment, no library, no accreditation, and no endowment. They had simply the self-confident belief in an idea. The resignations by faculty members in support of Sparling were acts of faith and idealism; indeed, several faculty members had made arrangements to mortgage their homes to support their new institution.

On December 17, 1945, the Dean of Faculties, Wayne Leys, reflected the enthusiasm, confidence, and pride of the university community in his report to the Board of Trustees:

> If it is foolhardy for 68 men [and a significant number of women] to resign their jobs without assurance of future security, the faculty of Roosevelt College was foolhardy.

1945 The first home of Roosevelt College was a nondescript building across from the el tracks at the corner of Wells and Quincy streets.

At the dedication of Roosevelt College, Eleanor Roosevelt, shown with President Edward J. Sparling, declared that the new school would "provide educational opportunities for persons of both sexes and of various races on equal terms."

If it is impossible to remodel an 11-story building in 33 days, equipping it with classrooms, library, laboratories, and offices, Roosevelt College was an impossibility.

If it is absurd for a new college to offer such subjects as advanced calculus, to apply for accreditation 6 days after the opening of school, and to graduate a class at the end of the first 17 weeks, then Roosevelt College is absurd. If it is radical to teach future labor leaders, as well as future business men, the mysteries of accounting; if it is radical to supply Jews, Poles, Japanese, and Negroes as well as Anglo-Saxons with the tools of language, then Roosevelt College is radical.

If it is impractical to give employed men and women during the evening hours courses of standard quality in history, chemistry, and music, Roosevelt College is impractical.

I am proud to say that Roosevelt College is in these ways foolhardy, impossible, absurd, radical, and impractical.

Roosevelt College found its first home at 231 South Wells Street, in an old loft that was scarcely the ideal setting for a college, but it was available at an extremely inexpensive price. Roosevelt was desperate for financial support. Sparling approached Edwin Embree, director of the Rosenwald Foundation, which had followed in the spirit of its founder, Julius Rosenwald, the CEO of Sears Roebuck, and supported black education for many years; he received $75,000. Then he was introduced to the philanthropist Marshall Field III, who befriended the fledgling institution and served on its Board of Trustees during those early, experimental years. "Without Marshall Field," Leo Lerner, a trustee and later chairman of the board, would remember, "Roosevelt University could not have been founded. I will never forget the day we had our first board meeting. It was a crucial meeting at a crucial moment. We needed 50,000 dollars to meet our first faculty payroll. Very quietly, Mr. Field said 'Go ahead. Sign the contract. I'll give you the money.'"

Fifteen hundred students from 40 states and 15 countries enrolled that first fall semester. On the 16th of November 1945, Eleanor Roosevelt dedicated the

Wells Street

The Wells Street campus of Roosevelt College soon became crowded with eager faces thirsting to be educated in an environment where a person is judged on merit only.

Dedicated to the Enlightenment of the Human Spirit

Central photo:

It was standing room only when this group of happy students attended Roosevelt's first assembly in September of 1945. And for good reason. The college had just moved into its new home at 231 S. Wells Street. The former office building had been remodeled to provide classrooms, library, laboratories, and offices in only 33 days.

Below, from left:

Wayne Leys, dean of Faculties, advises the first five students to register at Roosevelt College for the Fall quarter of 1945.

Though sparse, the Wells Street building did contain the all-important soda fountain, providing a lively place to pause, refresh, and meet.

Just as Roosevelt College was opening its doors for the first time, servicemen from World War II were beginning to return home by the thousands. They were happy to discover that a new college, named after their commander-in-chief, had been founded in Chicago. Howard G. Winebrenner, Roosevelt's director of admissions, was a busy man helping veterans to register under the provisions of the G.I. Bill.

college in her husband's name at a dinner in the Stevens Hotel, now the Hilton Chicago, before 1,000 people: "Roosevelt College of Chicago," she announced, "was founded to 'provide educational opportunities for persons of both sexes and of various races on equal terms'; and to maintain a teaching faculty which is both free and responsible in the discovery and dissemination of truth." Later she would describe the mission of this new institution: "Roosevelt University is dedicated to the enlightenment of the human spirit." If Franklin D. Roosevelt represented the pragmatic aspect of the university and its embodiment of his "four freedoms," Eleanor was the avatar of social justice and idealism – and so the Roosevelts, in a kind of democratic and moral diptych, spoke for the pragmatic idealism that would become the university's hallmark.

The importance of social justice and equality of opportunity to the young university cannot be overstated. In 1945, many colleges and universities demanded the religion, mother's maiden name, or name of all four grandparents on their applications for appointment. When private colleges and universities advertised for faculty positions, they often noted they were a "Christian organization" or a "Methodist organization" and Jews knew that meant they need not apply. At Roosevelt in the 1940's and 1950's there were at least twelve refugees from Nazi Europe, including the future third president of the university, Rolf Weil; then there were distinguished African-American scholars, like St. Clair Drake, Percy Julian, and Lorenzo Turner. The young institution appointed board members and hired highly qualified faculty who were not welcomed by other institutions. In 1948, an assistant professor of economics, Sara Landau, herself a refugee from Hitler, captured the spirit of Roosevelt in an article, "This School Bars None":

> There is a sense of living in a free world which can be matched by few schools in this or any other country, as I knew them. This does not mean that every faculty member and every student is liberal, tolerant or a near-god. But there is no sense of fear. There is assurance that

---

> There is a sense of living in a free world which can be matched by few schools in this or any other country, as I knew them.
>
> SARA LANDAU
> ASSISTANT PROFESSOR OF ECONOMICS
> 1948

your colleagues who are different also respect you as an individual and as a fellow citizen. Students, too, differ with each other and with some of us from time to time. But freedom from fear is here, and freedom of speech is here, and freedom of assembly is here.

Sparling was the dominant figure in those early years – a courageous, impatient idealist and risk taker whose moral convictions informed the institution. He had studied at Stanford and then Columbia, receiving his doctorate in secondary education. He was not an academic leader in the traditional sense, no scholar or teacher, but rather a public figure who represented Roosevelt to the labor unions and liberal organizations of the city. His intellectual conscience was Wayne Leys, who began his career as an associate pastor of the First Christian Church in Bloomington, Indiana, then served as chairman of the philosophy department at the YMCA College and became dean of faculty at Roosevelt College. Highly regarded by his peers and a modest man who authored many books, the best known of which was *Ethics for Policy Decisions* (1952), Leys was considered "the academic mind of Roosevelt" and a superb administrator. He and Sparling complemented each other, and they were supported by a gifted faculty who had fled discrimination in foreign lands and American cities and found an academic home in this new college.

It soon became apparent that the facilities on Wells Street were too small for the rapidly expanding institution. Sparling learned that the great Auditorium Building at Michigan Avenue and Congress Parkway, which had been created by the architect Louis Sullivan and engineer Dankmar Adler in 1889, was empty and available – an abandoned white elephant in the center of the city.

One of the most important and impressive architectural structures in the world, the Auditorium had enjoyed a colorful history, first as a ten-story hotel on Michigan Avenue and an office building on Wabash Avenue, with the magnificent Auditorium Theatre rising six stories within its core and a tower where

1947 When it moved into the Auditorium Building, Roosevelt's campus became Grant Park, enabling students to enjoy the beautiful flowers and fountains.

A New Home

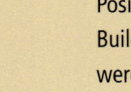

Ever the visionary, Edward J. Sparling saw, in the intrinsic beauty of this old, dusty, and neglected building, a new home for his growing student population.

Dedicated to the Enlightenment of the Human Spirit

Central photo:

Posing in front of the Auditorium Building are the two men who were largely instrumental in the founding of Roosevelt College – President Edward Sparling and Dean Wayne Leys. When enrollment growth could no longer be contained at the Wells Street campus, Sparling acquired the neglected Dankmar Adler and Louis Sullivan designed Auditorium Building, considered by experts to be one of the most important and impressive architectural structures in the world.

Below at right:

Posters advertised some of the many music and theatre productions that took place on the Auditorium Theatre stage during its heyday.

When the Great Depression came, the Auditorium Building and the theatre within it suffered hard times, and in 1939 closed down. During World War II, the building was taken over by the City of Chicago and used as a Servicemen's Center. Bowling alleys were constructed on the Auditorium Theatre stage where Adelina Patti, Enrico Caruso, Sarah Bernhardt, Anna Pavlova, and other famous artists performed. By the end of the war, over a million G.I.'s had been fed and entertained at the center or stayed overnight in rooms formerly occupied by presidents, royalty and the social elite.

Louis Sullivan had his office toward the end of his career. There was a long bar on Congress Parkway until the boulevard was widened for traffic that rushed in from the western suburbs. There were stories of President Benjamin Harrison's inauguration in 1889 and Theodore Roosevelt's Bull Moose convention in 1912, of Sarah Bernhardt reserving a hotel suite for her personal use, of Enrico Caruso and other classical stars performing in the Auditorium Theatre, of Frank Lloyd Wright – a protégé of Louis Sullivan and his young draftsman when the building was being designed – standing on the stage and reminding the audience to "be kind to this theater and it will be kind to you." The Chicago Symphony Orchestra performed in the theater until it moved to Orchestra Hall at 220 South Michigan Avenue in 1906; the Lyric Opera of Chicago presented there until it located in the Civic Opera House on Wacker Drive in 1929. When the economic depression came, the Auditorium Building and the theater within it suffered hard times and in 1939 closed down. During World War II, the stage of the Auditorium Theatre was used for bowling and other spaces for the accommodation of G.I.'s. There was serious consideration of demolishing what was considered by many people an architectural anachronism; but in 1946 the Auditorium Building was an attractive site for the administrators, faculty, and students of a new college searching for an academic home.

The building cost $85,000 and had accumulated taxes, all of which were forgiven when Roosevelt cooperated with the city's decision to widen Congress Parkway and create an arcade of the structures between State Street and Michigan Avenue. Sparling and his colleagues were aware of the great building they had inherited and there are wonderful photographs, some of them reprinted in this book, of Sparling and his relatives, of Leni Weil, wife of Roosevelt's third president, and other gracious women and faculty and students sweeping and cleaning the building and making it into their own. For the rest of the century and into the next, they would seek to

1947 Shortly after Roosevelt took possession of the dilapidated Auditorium Building, Roosevelt students held a clean-up party to scrub the main staircase.

1948 Enrollment at Roosevelt College exploded from 1,300 students in 1945 to more than 5,000 in 1948, with approximately half studying under the G.I. Bill.

1947 To publicize a divisive wire wall that divided the Auditorium Building lobby in half, Roosevelt held a "Chicken Wire Party" which was featured in *Life* magazine. President Sparling joined the king and queen of the party to let people know the wall should come down.

1949 Both sides were happy when Abraham Teitelbaum (left), owner of the north end of the Auditorium Building, finally gave in to community pressure and agreed to sell his portion of the building to Roosevelt College and President Sparling.

convert this multi-purpose, 19th century hotel, office building and theater into a university – and its conversion would be one of the more striking examples of an academic community's homage to a great work of architecture and historical landmark.

Before they could fully possess the Auditorium Building, however, there was a brief contretemps with Abraham Teitelbaum, who owned 52 feet of the north end of the Auditorium Building. Teitelbaum, a well-known attorney who allegedly had done some tax work for Al Capone, wanted $800,000, but Roosevelt refused to pay. He then erected a barrier in the lobby and a no trespassing sign that separated the two sections; he would not allow anyone associated with the university on his side. One of the problems was that the heating plant was in Teitelbaum's portion of the building. Roosevelt held a chicken wire party with a king and queen dressed as farmers; Abba Lerner, a distinguished emigré professor, read palms, told fortunes, and dressed like an old Jewish merchant; Sparling was in overalls and a straw hat; and the comical collection of students and faculty presented the royalty with a live chicken and gave chickens at the door as prizes. This party was featured in *Life* magazine as "Life Goes to a Party."

Teitelbaum finally agreed to Roosevelt's offer of $402,000 and its willingness to take a mortgage for $250,000 that would be paid by February 26, 1950. In November 1949 Sparling told Teitelbaum there was only $190,000 available to discharge the mortgage and offered to pledge his personal savings for the balance. Teitelbaum broke down. He told Sparling he must really love this college if he were willing to do that. The *Chicago Tribune* quoted the attorney: "I think it [Roosevelt University] is an asset too, because it offers educational opportunities to any student regardless of his creed, color or nationality. So I'll take the $190,000 and make the $60,000 balance a contribution to the school."

The true origins of Roosevelt University are found in the students, faculty, administrators, trustees, and volunteers of the Sparling era.

Getting Together

Friendships forming, romances brewing… getting together becomes easy when the common desire is success fueled by the exuberance of youth.

Dedicated to the Enlightenment of the Human Spirit

Because of its policy of nondiscrimination, Roosevelt College was able to offer students an atmosphere free of racial and cultural prejudice which resulted in an easy mix of ideas and activities.

Central photo:

Morale was high among these initiates at a new and radical educational institution in Chicago. With World War II behind and a promising future ahead, students at this mid-forties Christmas party danced to the popular music of bandleaders such as Tommy Dorsey and Glenn Miller.

Pictured below at right:

Jazz was taking hold and any student capable of pounding out a hand-clapping tune was a welcome addition to student life.

Clever student publicists chartered a streetcar to tour the loop with banners to advertise the showing of student-held plays. Ticket proceeds were used to benefit the college.

Students were drawn to Roosevelt because it had no quotas, charged minimal tuition, and accepted part-time older students, most of whom came after a full day of work and often stopped to meet and enjoy a refreshment before class.

1947 Roosevelt's phenomenal growth in the early years meant that many professors, especially those teaching business, social sciences and humanities, had as many as 150 students in their classes.

Whatever their religion or race or profession or standing in life, they were informed by the passionate principle of social justice. They knew they were participating in the creation of a unique university when the liberal imagination in western civilization had been most severely challenged and needed reformation and reaffirmation. Emerging from a Second World War that had been marked by the assertion of Aryan supremacy and the Holocaust, they now possessed a university that could express their humanitarian values. Having lost years in the war, students hungered for an education in the liberal arts and sciences and in professional training that would prove to be a passport to their prosperity. They had grown up in a city of racial and religious segregation and now could study together in a spirit of ethnic harmony rare in universities. Many were veterans who were supported by the G.I. Bill that FDR had initiated.

The students were exceptionally gifted and motivated – "the most challenging, the most argumentative, the most alert I have ever had," as one faculty member put it. Students were drawn to Roosevelt because it had no quotas; it charged minimal tuition; it accepted part-time, older students. But they were most attracted to the new college because it welcomed them, regardless of their background.

"Roosevelt was there when I needed it." How true this statement, which has become a mantra for the university, was for so many of the students. A loan fund was immediately established. Many G.I.'s had to wait to receive subsistence pay due them from the Veteran's Administration. The stories of supported students are legion and that of Wayne Leys is typical: Veteran "x" returned home from the war to his five brothers and sisters to find that his ill grandmother occupied the only bed available. He found a room to rent with another veteran. While waiting for his government subsistence check, he was looking for a job and often came to school hungry. The man received a loan within 24 hours of Roosevelt's learning of his plight.

1948 An apple for the teacher apparently worked for these couples as two Roosevelt instructors (second and third people in the photo) announced their engagements to two Roosevelt students.

1948 Many of Chicago's future leaders began their careers at the progressive new college. Chicago's first black mayor, Harold Washington, was both vice president and president of the student senate.

There was at this financially vulnerable college a generosity of spirit, a freedom from bureaucracy and regulations, long remembered by its graduates.

By February 1949, registration had reached 6,059 – 2,000 students were in a non-credit Labor Education Division and the credit-bearing Music School. Students took all of their courses in the Auditorium Building from 8:00 A.M. until 10:00 P.M., although most came after work. During this golden age so many future leaders of metropolitan Chicago emerged. Harold Washington became mayor of Chicago; his classmate, Dempsey Travis, developed a major real estate business and became a university trustee. Donald Jacobs rose to become dean of the Kellogg School of Management at Northwestern University. Some of the current trustees were students from the forties through the seventies: Myron Berkson, Clark Burrus, Norman Frankel, Alvin Golin, Joseph Hanauer, James Miller, Robert Mednick, Lance Poulsen, Seymour Persky, Manfred Steinfeld, Kenneth Tucker, Robert Wieseneck, and Edward Williams. Others – Elliot Eisner, Alonzo Crim – became educational leaders. Performing arts celebrities such as Benny Goodman, Jack Benny, Irene Dunne, Jeffrey Siegel, William Mason, Ramsey Lewis, and Herbie Hancock are among the graduates and long-term students of the Chicago Musical College. Police chiefs – Leroy Martin, Frederick Rice, Matthew Rodriguez – studied at Roosevelt. Teachers whose names may not be so well known took their professional preparation into the classrooms of the Chicago Public Schools. The city government is anchored by many Roosevelt graduates. The list is long, the list is distinguished. It includes a wide range of people who have lived and worked in metropolitan Chicago. Indeed 80% of the university's graduates live in this immediate region – and when one sets aside international students, the percentage is even higher. In ways immeasurable Roosevelt has been a university for Chicagoans.

Inspired Faculty

Inspired by the passionate principle of social justice, students could study and faculty could teach in a spirit of ethnic harmony rare in universities at the time.

Dedicated to the Enlightenment of the Human Spirit

It was with enthusiasm, confidence and pride that the faculty of this nascent college gathered for an early meeting. Many of these individuals resigned their positions with the YMCA College, and, without assurance of future security, followed Edward J. Sparling in the formation of Roosevelt College. Among the full-time faculty in 1946 were a substantial number of refugees from the Nazis, Afro-American scholars who could not find employment in traditional institutions and several Asians.

Also there at the beginning was Rolf Weil, later to become Roosevelt's third president. In his book, *Through These Portals*, Weil writes:
"Referring to the objectives and underlying philosophy of Roosevelt, President Sparling said in his 1947-48 President's Report, 'we do not mean to imply that equality of opportunity is the same thing as education for everybody but we have successfully affirmed in practice the theory that all students who can profit by a college education should have the equal privilege of obtaining a college education.'"

1 Edward J. Sparling	12 Wayne A. R. Leys	23 Kendall Taft	34	45 Estelle DeLacy
2 Marjorie C. Keenleyside	13 Warren P. Cortelyou	24 Richard J. Hooker	35	46
3 Harland H. Allen	14	25 Dale Pontius	36 Benedict Mayer	47
4 Samuel Spechthrie	15 Emanuel Merdinger	26 Hermann C. Bowersox	37	48
5 Saul Dorfman	16 Otto Wirth	27 Henry C. Johnson	38 Robert Runo	49
6 Joseph Creanza	17 Edward Robbins	28 Millard Everett	39	50
7 Arthur Hillman	18 Frank Untermyer	29 Emery W. Balduf	40 Hans Tischler	51
8 Lowell Huelster	19	30 George Watson	41	52 Conroy Lawson
9 Carlisle Bloxom	20	31	42	53
10 Edward Chandler	21	32 G. D. Gore	43 Margaret Williams	54 Gustav Dunkelberger
11 Thomas A. Hart	22 Rolf A. Weil	33 Jacob Hirning	44	

Administrators and Faculty

In the university's infancy, certain administrators and faculty shaped its character. Jim Sparling and Wayne Leys were clearly the principal leaders, but others defined Roosevelt in their own ways and gave it a special character that reflected the America Walt Whitman once described: Roosevelt University was, like America itself, a "nation of nations."

Otto Wirth was a German immigrant who came to the U.S. in 1932 and received the Bronze Star for service during World War II. At Roosevelt, he was a professor of languages, dean of faculties, and vice president of academic affairs. Wirth established the cultural studies department in order to promote international and inter-racial relations and began his description of the department by stating that "an improved understanding of diverse cultures should reduce intercultural fear or rivalry." Later Wirth was awarded the Distinguished Service Award from the alumni association – "for his humility, his learning, his concern for scholarship and the functions of the mind." He was inducted into Chicago's Senior Citizens Hall of Fame.

Wayne Leys

Otto Wirth

Joseph Creanza

Arthur Hillman

Abba Lerner

Joseph Creanza was a fiery idealist, a professor of modern languages at the Central YMCA College who had immediately followed Sparling's resignation with his own. So passionately did Creanza share Sparling's intention of creating a new college that he offered to mortgage his own house to help finance the purchase. Although Creanza was not a performing artist, he cared deeply about music and was the key figure in negotiating the acquisition of the Chicago Music College in 1954 and became its first director. A few years later, he was instrumental in the efforts to restore the Auditorium Theatre.

Arthur Hillman was chairman of the Urban Studies Program and served as dean of arts and sciences. He received his PhD in sociology and social service administration from the University of Chicago in 1946 and went on to become director of the National Federation of Settlements and Neighborhood Centers.

The child of refugees from Nazi Germany, Rolf Weil joined the economics department in 1946 while completing his doctoral dissertation at the University of Chicago. He became dean of the business college and then was appointed president of Roosevelt University in 1965. For 23 years he remained in that office, and his influence on the university was profound. The second chapter of this history is devoted to the Weil presidency, one that took a vulnerable institution that had difficulty balancing its budget and stabilized it financially.

1954 Rolf Weil joined Roosevelt in 1946 as a 24-year-old assistant professor of economics. Although he later became dean of the business college and president of the university, his first love remains teaching. Since his retirement in 1988, he has taught "Money and Banking" at the Chicago Campus.

Walter Weisskopf was the highly regarded chairman of the Economics Department and an academic leader as well as long-time board member. A scholar with a national reputation, he was the author of *The Psychology of Economics*.

Weisskopf brought to the university Abba Lerner. Lerner was a native of Russia who had grown up on the lower East End of London and attended the London School of Economics, where he was one of the most brilliant students. He spent three years in the 1950's in Israel as an economic advisor to the government, the Ministry of Finance, and the Bank of Israel. A prolific author of books and essays on economy theory, inflation, and unemployment, Lerner was a major participant in the Institute for Mediterranean Affairs.

St. Clair Drake – John Gibbs St. Clair Drake Jr. – became a professor of sociology in 1946. When Roosevelt College was established, Drake had already accepted a position as a social worker in New York City, but Arthur Hillman, Chairman of the Sociology Department, visited him there and persuaded him to join the faculty, where he promptly became a star. The son of a Barbadian sailor who jumped ship in Virginia and became an African Methodist

Episcopalian preacher in Pittsburgh, St. Clair Drake had settled into Chicago and written a small classic for the WPA. He graduated from college and studied Ghandhian non-violent resistance at the Quaker Graduate Centre in Pennsylvania. At Roosevelt, in 1946, Drake, Lorenzo Turner, and Frank Untermyer developed one of the first African Studies programs in the country. St. Clair Drake became one of the most influential and important sociologists of his time. With others, he published "Deep South: A Social Anthropological Study of Caste and Class."

He was a member of the training staff of the Peace Corps teams that went to Ghana in the early 1960's, and in 1962 he presided over the conference of West African social workers, held in Ghana. His classic study, written with Horace Cayton, is *Black Metropolis: a Sociology Study of Chicago's Black Community*,

1952 Sociologist St. Clair Drake was one of Roosevelt's most distinguished professors and scholars. He wrote extensively on the topics of race and class.

published in 1945 and reviewed on page 1 of *The New York Times Book Review* by Louis Wirth of the University of Chicago. Louis Wirth was the brother of Otto Wirth, who ultimately became Dean of Faculties of Roosevelt University. That book review resulted in attracting at least one new member of the faculty to a teaching career at Roosevelt.

The exchange of notable English scholars became a way of life at Roosevelt. The one who made the greatest impact was Harold Laski of the London School of Economics. Laski delivered five lectures on American politics before packed audiences, and the "Laski Lectures" became famous in Chicago.

Edwin Turner

Tarini Sinha

Frank Untermyer

Edwin Turner was the only black college basketball coach of an integrated college team. He also coached soccer, softball, track, basketball, bowling, track, tennis, and golf – although he was not allowed on private golf courses when his own team played. A gentle man, Turner told one of his former players, Ira Berkow – who has become the senior sports writer for the *New York Times* – that he did not protest because he cared too much for the team; nor did he get angry because he "would not have been able to think clearly."

Tarini P. Sinha, professor of economics and political science, was educated at the Hindu University, Benares, and the University of London. A personal friend of Ghandi and Tagore, Sinha had a charismatic effect on his students; he died of a cerebral hemorrhage on December 2, 1946. The students were so affected by him during his short life that they dedicated the first yearbook of Roosevelt College to him, citing his "unique faculty for involving himself with each of [their] lives."

Frank Untermyer was a professor of political science with special interest in African culture and has taught or consulted at Roosevelt for its entire history. His father was a distinguished jurist in New York and with the funds he inherited, Untermyer was for many years the university's most generous "anonymous" donor, supporting minority students in their work and never taking credit for his benevolence. Only recently has he allowed his name to be associated with his extraordinary philanthropy, which by now has amounted to many millions of dollars.

Rudolph Ganz was brought to the United States from Zurich, Switzerland in 1901 by Florenz Ziegfeld, founder and first president of the Chicago Musical College [CMC] which he had established in 1867. After a distinguished career of concertizing and a period as conductor of the symphony orchestra in St. Louis, Ganz returned to CMC in 1929 and became president as well as head of the piano department. Ganz was instrumental in having CMC become one of the standing colleges of Roosevelt

University in 1954. It now has 400 students and has combined with the theater program of 200 students to form a Chicago College of the Performing Arts, with conservatories in music and theater. In addition to a brilliant faculty, it now has 25 principal players from the Chicago Symphony Orchestra and the Lyric Opera as master teachers. The major concert room, used constantly for student and faculty performances, is Ganz Hall, named after the College's guiding spirit, this most distinguished international musical figure, Rudolph Ganz.

Trustees

Edwin Embree was the first chairman of the board of trustees. As the head of the Rosenwald Foundation, he was responsible for authorizing a $75,000 contribution to Roosevelt College. Without this gift, the college would never have been established.

Leo Lerner was a founding trustee and chairman of the board for ten years. A native of a south side slum where his father was an Austrian immigrant, he became the president of Lerner newspapers, which published 21 community papers. A short, outspoken champion of liberal causes, Lerner left his mark on Roosevelt College: "He used one and two syllable words with penetrating effect," as one colleague remarked. "Lerner has sought to introduce democracy to the common man through the kitchen door." He regularly taught a course in journalism, the first of its kind in the university. A leader of many progressive causes, Leo Lerner helped to organize the Independent Voters of Illinois. In 1961, at a tempestuous and seminal meeting (described on page 41), he fought against the university's opening of the Auditorium Theatre and resigned in protest. But when he was at Roosevelt his influence was very great indeed.

Percy Julian was an original trustee in 1945, the first African-American board member of a college that was not exclusively black. Julian had no formal education as a consequence of Southern laws and was taught at home by his parents; he was first in his

> It is a very mixed-up world, but the only one; and there is only one race: the human race.
>
> ELEANOR ROOSEVELT
> IN A TALK AT ROOSEVELT UNIVERSITY

class at DePauw University and earned a master's degree with distinction from Harvard University. He founded Julian Laboratories in 1953 and was responsible for many scientific discoveries, ranging from treatment for rheumatoid arthritis to glaucoma. At Roosevelt's dedication he underscored the mission of the fledgling institution:

> Roosevelt College is neither pro-labor nor pro-management; it is neither pro-Negro nor pro-white; it is neither pro-Jewish nor pro-Gentile – it is instead a college wherein men and women are to learn that their real problems can only be solved if they sit down together around a common table and approach these problems without the pressure of fettered or biased opinion. Together we shall strive to teach nothing but the truth so help us God. This is the first and fundamental cornerstone of Roosevelt College.

Percy Julian

Leo Lerner

Harland Allen

Edwin Embree

Harland Allen was a Wall Street financier who predicted in the April 1929 issue of *Barron's* "the end of stock market enthusiasm by the fourth quarter of 1929." He organized the business college and became its dean from 1947 to 1949. From 1959 to 1963 he served as chairman of the board of trustees, during which time the university decided to restore the Auditorium Theatre.

John Roosevelt, the son of Franklin and Eleanor, served on the Board of Trustees from 1975 until his death in 1981.

Friends of Roosevelt University

The number of private citizens who were inspired by the meaning of Roosevelt University during the '40's and '50's is long and impressive. World War II, the Holocaust, the McCarthy era, the emerging racial revolution – these and other social phenomena created an inviting cultural context for a new, secular university free of discrimination. Among all of the university's advocates, however, three figures loom especially large.

As chairman of the board of Sears, Roebuck, & Co., Julius Rosenwald contributed significantly toward education in the south, establishing the

1950 A scroll commemorating the college's founders was examined by (from left) President Sparling, trustee Marshall Field III and Harold Ickes, second chairman of the Board of Trustees.

Pianist Rudolph Ganz was associated with Chicago Musical College from 1927 until his death in 1972 at the age of 95. During most of those years, he was president of CMC. He also was conductor of the St. Louis Symphony Orchestra and a composer of 250 titles.

Rosenwald Foundation in 1917 to aid in the medical, economic, and cultural advancement of African-Americans. In the spirit of Rosenwald's philanthropy and as president of the foundation, Edwin Embree contributed the initial $75,000 gift that made Roosevelt College a possibility.

Marshall Field III, grandson of the Marshall Field who established the department store, was an original trustee and founder of Roosevelt. Most of his vast fortune was in support of social causes. It was his gift of $50,000 that allowed Roosevelt to meet its first payroll. Field was an admirer of Franklin Roosevelt and the New Deal. He started *The Sun* in 1941, which later merged with *The Times*, to give Chicago its daily liberal newspaper, *The Sun-Times*, in the 1950's and 1960's.

Eleanor Roosevelt was more of a symbolic than an actual figure in the birth and development of the university. Although she came to Roosevelt only several times, she drew support from Albert Einstein, Pearl Buck, Albert Schweitzer, Thomas Mann, and Ralph Bunche – all of whom lent their names to the only institution of higher learning in America that bore her husband's name. One of the most admired figures of the twentieth century, Eleanor Roosevelt represented the university's commitment to social justice, racial equality, and pragmatism. Years later, a Franklin and Eleanor Roosevelt Center for Democratic Values would be established that included a Mansfield Institute for Social Justice, a St. Clair Drake Center for African and African-American Affairs, a Center for New Deal Studies, and an Institute for Metropolitan Affairs; in addition, a relationship would be forged with the Franklin and Eleanor Roosevelt Institute in Hyde Park, where the Roosevelt library resides, and an annual lecture established under the leadership of Mrs. Roosevelt's grand-daughter, Anna Roosevelt.

These fabulous founders, these original trustees, faculty, administrators, students, and friends – these "happy warriors" (to borrow FDR's phrase) – who ignited an idea and an institution represented an aggressive spirit that combined Jeffersonian "natural aristocracy" – the highest academic standards, regardless of religious or racial origins, social liberalism, pragmatism, and entrepreneurship. The children of immigrants, the grandchildren of slaves, veterans who emerged from the neighborhoods of Chicago, faculty who had fled Nazi Germany, and young people from every religion, race and ethnic group in Chicago, America, and the world formed the clear image of Roosevelt College. It was a unique American college of the post-war era and became a university in the early '50's, as business, music and other professional programs were developed. By 1954 it was Roosevelt University, settled in the Auditorium Building at Congress Parkway and Michigan Avenue, a Chicago institution at its core.

Nowhere was the democratic spirit of the university better expressed than in its governance. The president and five faculty, a committee that handled all administrative matters, served on a board of trustees comprised of two-thirds members. Every faculty member, including part-timers, voted on all issues. There was a provision for a vote of confidence every three years that needed to receive a two-thirds vote of affirmation from colleagues in their divisions and a majority from the entire faculty in order for administrative leaders to be reappointed. Fortunately, the two-thirds rule, which was advisory in any case, was never applied. Two students participated in faculty meetings and had a vote on eight of the faculty committees. Half of the important Budget Committee, responsible to the Board of Trustees for the formulation of a balanced budget, were faculty elected by the University Senate. It would be many years before the modern separation of authority among trustees, administration, faculty, and students developed, although the elements of shared governance still persist. Roosevelt remains a university remarkably open in its decision making. Even though this practice can lead to slower resolutions, it also results in fewer crises between faculty and administration.

From Top:

1949 This plaque was a gift from the Class of 1949.

1959 Eleanor Roosevelt attended a black tie dinner at which Roosevelt University was rededicated to both her husband, Franklin Delano Roosevelt, and her. Board Chairman Leo Lerner and President Sparling joined her in showing off the new plaque.

1954 Just three years after it first began offering graduate courses in 1951, Roosevelt College declared itself a university. In 1955, the North Central Association of Colleges and Schools confirmed the change.

1950's For many years, Roosevelt College was closely aligned with organized labor. More than 50 international unions enrolled their members in the Labor Education Division to take non-credit courses on such topics as collective bargaining, union administration and the history of labor.

The democratic spirit that infused the university was also expressed by its commitment to labor education. Sparling's public support of labor was one of the reasons why he was at odds with the Central YMCA board. Trustees had criticized him for tolerating discussions on racial, religious, and labor problems within the YMCA College, and when he suggested that the college should service labor in the community as it had long supported business they turned him down. Board members did not like the liberal organizations to which Sparling belonged, among them the Pan-American Good Neighbor Forum, which promoted interracial good will with Latin America and the Independent Voters of Illinois. Many of the misgivings the directors had concerning Sparling's public behavior culminated in speeches he delivered at a meeting of the union that was on strike against Montgomery Ward.

Frank W. McCullough was a key figure in the establishment of Roosevelt College. Leon Despres, McCullough's close friend and a liberal lawyer and alderman, reports that three men assembled together during the crisis that led to its birth: Jim Sparling, Frank McCullough, and Leo Lerner. "They might have fitted into a telephone booth if it had not been for Leo," remarked McCullough, in an obvious reference to Leo Lerner's rather expansive girth. McCullough founded Roosevelt's non-credit Labor Education Division, which trained shop stewards and union members who had little previous education in positions of secondary leadership and offered courses in collective bargaining, union administrative methods, and labor history. The International Ladies' Garment Workers' Union, the United Auto Workers, the Almagamated Clothing Workers, and the American Federation of State, County and Municipal Employees [AFSCME] were among the unions participating in the program. These activities were represented by a prominent place in the curriculum and by community projects that identified Roosevelt for many years as a university strongly sympathetic to labor.

The pro-labor position of the university helped to create the image of Roosevelt as "the little red school house" during the 1950's, when Senator Joseph McCarthy was conducting his hearings of those who may have belonged to the communist party. Of course, the typical Roosevelt student was scarcely ideological – he wanted an education that would prepare him for a career. The faculty was predominately liberal and there were one or two "fellow travelers," those who sympathized with communism and may or may not have been party members. The majority of the Roosevelt community, however, was free of ideology and fundamentally struggling to survive financially and build a university.

The community continued, of course, to be sensitive to issues of social justice. One of the incidents that typifies the period was the introduction by Illinois Senator Broyles, head of the Seditious Activities Committee, of anti-communist bills. Students from Roosevelt and the University of Chicago motorcaded to Springfield and picketed Broyles' office. Broyles was furious and told his secretary to discover what schools the students were from. He then persuaded the state legislature to investigate communism at both Roosevelt and the University of Chicago. An investigator visited Dean Wayne Leys and asked about communism at Roosevelt, whereupon Leys took him to the library and showed him the books about communism and the many more books concerned with American democracy. Sparling himself appeared before the Broyles Commission and stressed the moderate views of the Roosevelt community. The Commission accused St. Clair Drake of having been part of a black activist organization suspected of being pro-communist, to which Sparling responded that if the commission members only knew St. Clair Drake they wouldn't have to ask.

Roosevelt students often protested discrimination in its various forms. Before Roosevelt was even established, several members of the Social Action Group had been arrested at the White City Roller Rink, which did not admit blacks, when they refused

1950 The candles tell the story. President Sparling cuts a cake celebrating the fifth anniversary of Roosevelt College.

Hungry Minds

Students hungered for an education in the liberal arts and sciences and in professional training that would be a passport to their prosperity.

Dedicated to the Enlightenment of the Human Spirit

The culturally pluralistic environment at Roosevelt created a stimulating atmosphere for teaching and learning. The students were exceptionally gifted and motivated – "the most challenging, the most argumentative, the most alert I have ever had," as one faculty member put it.

Central photo:

Revenue from increasing enrollments allowed the university to properly equip its science labs with the latest teaching aids, as shown in Professor Bernard Greenberg's 1959 biology class.

Pictured below from left:

Making papier-mache masks is one of the projects these future teachers must master in the "Arts and Crafts in the Elementary School" course taught by Donald Baum (standing). A large percentage of Roosevelt University graduates have gone on to teach in the Chicago Public Schools.

Warm weather provided Professor Morris Goran with the opportunity to conduct his Physical Science class on Roosevelt's front yard – Grant Park.

Professor of Sociology St. Clair Drake's classes were very popular. He was instrumental in developing one of the first African Studies programs in the country.

1945 Roosevelt students helped raise money for their college by holding fundraising events like this one, which featured entertainment, music and guest speakers.

to move from the ticket window until a black in line was sold a ticket…On one occasion in the 1950's, they held a "D-Day." The date was kept a secret and all students and faculty had to abide by the rules. Blondes and people with small heads were not allowed in the library and men with mustaches were barred from the elevator…A student filed a lawsuit against a company that reneged on a job after discovering she was black. Roosevelt students attended the trial when she won the case…Students held a five-minute vigil three days in a row to protest the bombing of a church and the slaying of at least six children and two youths in Birmingham, Alabama. Sparling permitted registration to be halted during the time.…In 1962 students participated in demonstrations at Congress Parkway and Michigan Avenue to protest the resumption of atmospheric nuclear testing by the U.S.

The identification with labor, the progressive university programs throughout the 1950's, and the minimal membership of corporate leaders on the board of trustees created a distance between the university and the business community. Most companies were led by wealthy, white, Christian men who served on the boards of the Art Institute, Lyric Opera, and other cultural institutions or they were trustees of the University of Chicago, Northwestern, and other institutions that had very few blacks and Jews as students, either through overt quotas in admissions or through benign neglect. Business leaders viewed Roosevelt's non-discrimination policy as an indication of a left-wing faculty and resisted supporting the university. Sparling had to turn to Jewish businessmen like Leo Lerner of the Lerner newspapers, the Hillmans of the grocery store chain, and Sam Booth, a furniture wholesaler.

In addition, there was a rigid hierarchy among foundations and corporations in terms of philanthropy to universities. It descended from the University of Chicago and Northwestern to Loyola, DePaul and lesser institutions. Because of its infancy, its liberal impulses, and its lack of corporate titans on the board, Roosevelt was near the bottom of this list. As Sparling often said, during the first sixteen years of the university, he and his colleagues were literally moving from one financial crisis to another. Only because the back taxes and penalties were either paid or forgiven was the university able to meet the rising educational needs of its community. Except for the Rosenwald Foundation and Marshall Field, it would not be until the Weil administration in the mid-sixties that an overt effort was made to solicit funds from major foundations and corporations; and it would not be until my presidency that a younger generation of donors and foundation leaders would consider proposals in terms of their inherent merits rather than their institutional identification. The segregation of class, race, and religion affected Roosevelt University in profound ways until the revolutions of the '60's, and the university was not recognized in philanthropic circles until the '70's.

Jerome Stone, who would become a major volunteer leader of the university and chairman of the board of trustees for fifteen years, remembered the early tension between the university and the business community most vividly in a speech he delivered in 1990:

"But there were difficult times, as is true of all new boys on the block and since Roosevelt was different from the normal collegiate pattern in its student body and administration, it was viewed with some suspicion by conservative elements in Chicago. In fact, on LaSalle Street, the College was branded left wing. Part of their problem was the idealism of our founding president, Jim Sparling. They didn't understand that our greatest strength was the richness of our racial, ethnic and cultural diversity. Sparling was never able to connect the pragmatism to these ideals to make a welcome combination for all of Chicago.

"When I was importuned to come on the board, I remember that Leo Lerner, then chairman, pointed out to me that it was important for the businessmen on the board to explain the university to the business community...."

1950's Unpacking merchandise for the grand opening of "The Scholarshop," members of the Women's Scholarship Association, including Mrs. Sparling (center), discuss effective display methods.

1940's Students organized a wide variety of activities in the early years, including the glamorous Miss Roosevelt College pageant.

"In the late 1950's, a good friend of the university, Laird Bell, who had also been chairman of the board of the University of Chicago, offered to call a meeting of the power structure of the business community, and asked that Walter Heller, who was not a board member but a friend, and I explain the university to the group (as he put it) in business terms, or what it meant to Chicago and its business and social community. Incidentally, he also advised me that it was important Jim Sparling not be at this meeting because he, too, had to be explained to this august gathering.

"In walking into that room at the Chicago Club and meeting for the first time some 15 distinguished leaders and power brokers of the city was, to put it mildly, a somewhat unnerving experience. Walter Heller spoke first and pointed out in his usual terse but clear terms, 'Gentlemen, this is a university that is here to stay; if you don't support it, it will still be here. If you do, it will probably be the best urban university in the country.'

"When I spoke, I pointed out that our company, like the university, had started out with a dream of success; that the university was an institution like a company starting out small, probably under financed, but by its ideals and practicality was educating 6,000 students with no prejudices and giving them opportunities that every American could appreciate. It was indeed an American saga, a story of success in the best traditions and one that you gentlemen can appreciate because it didn't have a great benefactor and the students paid over 90% of the going cost of the university.

"After Walter and I spoke, they spoke amongst themselves. They were really like the bourbon kings of old, knowing only what their courtesans had told them. Finally, Homer Pettibone, at that time chairman of the Chicago Title and Trust Co., said: 'Gentlemen, we have heard two inspirational talks today which utterly contradict all that we have heard before at this club, and any other gathering when we've had the opportunity to talk about this school. I'm going to give this young fellow $5,000 to get a public relations program started to tell the story that these 2 men enlightened us with today.' It was an interesting meeting."

When Sullivan and Adler created the Auditorium Building, with its hotel on Michigan Avenue and Congress Parkway and its offices on Wabash Avenue, they located the 4,200-seat Auditorium Theatre, six stories high, in its core. Commerce would sustain culture, they reasoned, but with the Great Depression of the twenties and the movement of the Chicago Symphony Orchestra and Lyric Opera elsewhere in the city, neither business nor art could support a magnificent theater that ultimately came to be considered an albatross. The Auditorium Building and especially the Auditorium Theatre fell on hard times and when Roosevelt took them over in 1946 they were in a state of disrepair. The tension between business and art would manifest itself during the 1950's at Roosevelt as Sparling sought to merge the Chicago Musical College into the university and then resurrect the Auditorium Theatre, just as he had the Auditorium Building. Out of his struggle developed the first great crisis of the young university and one that persisted, at different levels of intensity, for the next fifty years.

In 1954 the Chicago Musical College [CMC], which had originally been founded in 1867 by Florenz Ziegfeld Sr., was in financial straits. Joseph Creanza worked assiduously toward the acquisition of CMC, noting the international prestige of its president, Rudolph Ganz, and the former status of CMC as one of the finest conservatories in the country. President Sparling championed the acquisition, although his Dean of Faculties, Wayne Leys, and his Vice President for Finance, Lowell Huelster, opposed it. Sparling persuaded the Board of Trustees to acquire CMC, and the College now became a University. CMC did run a deficit for the next 33 years and it was unfortunate that the prominence and prestige of Rudolph Ganz never resulted in significant fundraising. It was not until Earl Schub became dean of the College in 1987 that a strategic plan was forged, fundraising developed, and an annual gala organized by the Chicago Board of Roosevelt University that raised up to $1 million annually.

1889 The Auditorium Building, acquired by Roosevelt College in 1946, is recognized as one of the most important architectural structures in the world. When the building opened on December 9, 1889, it contained 17 million bricks, 50,000 square feet of marble, 800,000 square feet of terra-cotta, 60,000 square feet of plate glass, 25 miles of gas and water pipes and 10,000 electric lights. It cost $4 million to build.

> Every advance in knowledge and of intelligence has been and will be connected with increased responsibility and wider possibilities of shaping the condition of man's life.
>
> NIELS BOHR
> NOBEL-PRIZE-WINNING
> ATOMIC SCIENTIST, IN A TALK AT
> ROOSEVELT UNIVERSITY

A far deeper issue arose as Sparling contemplated the restoration of the Auditorium Theatre. It had remained dormant since the Second World War, when its stage became a bowling alley for the GIs, and was in extreme need of repair. During the 1950's there had been many suggestions about how this huge space – a theater that rose six stories high within the core of the building, had 4,200 seats, and occupied 40% of the Auditorium Building – might be used. As early as 1947, at Sparling's request, Joseph Creanza submitted a report that outlined three alternatives: (1) the Theatre could be rented to a commercial organization; (2) the College could operate the Theatre itself; or (3) a separate but not independent organization could be established and given the responsibility of operating the Theatre with a "city-center" type of cultural programming. Over the years, ideas ranged from tearing the Auditorium Theatre down and building a garage to using it as a student center. At one point, the National Broadcasting Company considered converting it into a space for national programming.

None of these proposals proved feasible and the theater was too expensive to demolish. Sparling saw the potentialities of the theater and wanted to make it into a great cultural forum for speakers, lecturers, and performing artists. He insisted that the College control the theater, claiming as early as November 16, 1949, in a report to the faculty, that it "would net us between $50,000 and $100,000 per year income – tax free. This would be equivalent to an endowment of anywhere from 1½ to 3 million dollars. Put another way, I feel that every dollar we invest in the Auditorium would be putting three to six additional dollars to work for us." Throughout the '50's and '60's the Auditorium Theatre became the most important, controversial, time-consuming and vexing issue to confront the University community. Roosevelt had severe financial concerns and any plan was disproportionate to the funds needed. Indeed, at the very time the Board of Trustees was considering a "globalization" campaign of $1.82 million, Sparling was advocating a fundraising drive of national proportions to restore this great landmark. Members of his own administration and faculty were divided on the issue; so were the trustees. Daniel Perlman, in a study of the governance of Roosevelt University completed in 1971, summarizes the tensions within the university:

Because all of the leadership figures of the institution had taken sides, compromise was exceedingly difficult. The issue aroused the loyalties and antipathies of those who felt close to or alienated from the president, the board chairman, the dean of faculties, or the vice-president for development, all of whom took strong positions on the matter. There was scarcely anyone of stature within the institution who did not come to be aligned with one or another of these positions or identified within one or another leadership figure. Consequently there were no neutral or uncommitted individuals who, with untarnished prestige, could work out a compromise acceptable to all.

There was a "cultural crisis" in Chicago at the time, occasioned by the Chicago Opera House, a venue for opera and ballet, being rented as a widescreen movie theater for ten months of each year. A former trustee, Arnold Maremont, proposed that the Metropolitan Fair and Exposition Authority restore the Auditorium Theatre in return for a long-term lease of 40 years at $50,000 per year. Leo Lerner, the Chairman of the Board, and another trustee, Robert Pollack, were strongly in favor of the proposal; but the Board opposed it, and followed the recommendation of President Sparling. "He very much wanted the University to control the Theatre," Perlman writes, "and to use it not only to derive income but to enhance and extend its cultural offerings and its public image. A University cultural center in the Theatre, he believed, would not only attract additional students but would attract additional contributions to support the University."

A survey by John Pierce Jones Co. was conducted to "study the implications of the architectural restoration of the Auditorium Theatre within the

1999 One hundred and ten years after the Auditorium Theatre opened, it was the premier venue in the Midwest for the presentation of Broadway shows like *Les Miserables, Phantom of the Opera, Miss Saigon,* and *Show Boat*.

The Jewel

A jewel in a magnificent setting, the resplendent Auditorium Theatre is at the core of the Auditorium Building

In stark contrast to the rather sober facade of the Auditorium Building is the ornate Auditorium Theatre, which rises six stories in height and occupies 40 percent of this massive structure. Golden in hue when alive with light, the theatre's soaring arches reach from the stage to contribute to nearly perfect acoustics.

Pictured below at right:

The decorative beauty of the Auditorium Theatre interior was demonstrated in advertising material through the use of photos and illustrations. These early images show the Congress Parkway lobby, the stage of the Auditorium Theatre, and the ornate metalwork of a theatre balcony box.

Dedicated to the Enlightenment of the Human Spirit

framework of the total restoration of the building as an architectural and acoustical masterpiece." The Jones report recommended that the theatre be restored but that an agency be established that was autonomous and independent. Sparling, however, would not relinquish control of the theater. As he had done when he resigned from the presidency of the Central YMCA College, he turned to the faculty for support; they were divided in their views, as were key figures in his own administration. Sparling then found Beatrice Spachner, who had helped to raise money for the renovated Ganz Hall and who was a trustee as well as a wealthy patron of the arts. She volunteered to restore the Auditorium Theatre.

Spachner was a determined woman and soon took on the Auditorium Theatre as her own cause, championing it until her death in 1981 and setting into motion a drama within the institution that lasted for the next four decades. She presented a compromise plan to the trustees, but they demanded that she prove that there was enough financial support from the public for the renovation and that no university funds be used. In July 1959 she reported that she had raised $500,000 in pledges and was given approval to proceed. But trustee endorsement came only after bitter dissension. Sparling was Spachner's chief advocate, but his vice president for academic affairs, John Golay, his vice president for development, Wells Burnette, and his graduate dean and former dean of faculties, Wayne R. Leys, all resigned under protest. Sparling also confronted strong opposition from his board chairman, Leo Lerner, who was sympathetic to the restoration of the Auditorium Theatre but felt that the university could not afford a fund drive that would inevitably draw donors away from the fundamental and pressing needs of the university. Sides were taken: those who supported Sparling, those

The Auditorium Theatre is as magnificent today as it was in the 1890's thanks to Beatrice Spachner who raised funds in the late 1950's and early 1960's to renovate the dilapidated facility.

who agreed with Lerner, and a middle group that sought compromise. For months the conflict raged on until Leo Lerner submitted his resignation at a stormy meeting on February 18, 1960:

…Now you vote this form of Auditorium adventure and ask the remaining Board members, those not on the Auditorium committee or what you call the Council, to raise the deficit against self-competition and all the other odds. The glamour pants will attempt to restore an unneeded theater (which will probably remain empty most of the time) and the drones are expected to raise the money for faculty salaries and student facilities. It won't work. Those who have given the best part of the last 15 years of their lives to help raise funds for the University can't be put into that position.

We refuse to go out on the street from door to door to look for money to keep the college going when the President and some of the Board members insist on going off on this fantastic tangent. This is a job that is difficult when everyone is co-operating. A last point. A Board of Trustees is supposed to be a deliberative body. But we have never deliberated the alternative possible uses of the Auditorium property. What about a gymnasium and a swimming pool for the students? What about a student union? Do we not owe any loyalty to our students? In the last two years, we have had only one choice. We could only vote "yes."

This is an an impossible atmosphere. A volunteer cannot work in it. There are other things to do in this world than remain on a board which would vote such an unbelievable legal document in the face of several opinions from reliable lawyers that it does not protect the university and is not sufficiently detailed to a workable contract for the future. As now constituted, it is a gift of 40% of the University's real property to person or persons unknown.

I regret very much, but I herewith resign from this Board.

God bless you all!

1961 The Founder's Day celebration attracted (from left) Supreme Court Justice Arthur Goldberg, ABC television commentator Howard K. Smith, Mrs. Marshall Field, President Sparling, trustee Percy Julian, Senator Charles Percy, and Board Chairman Harland Allen.

Lerner's resignation was followed by that of three other board members and a faculty trustee and received great public attention. Nevertheless, a compromise was fashioned that authorized Beatrice Spachner to create an Auditorium Theatre Council that would raise funds for restoration of the theater only and then manage it, subject to approval of the trustees. Board members were concerned that Sparling was so enthusiastic about the theater that he would divert his efforts in fundraising from the university to the theater and therefore had Beatrice Spachner report directly to them. By circumventing the administration of the university and separating fundraising for the theater from the university, the trustees sowed the seeds of separation. By not having the majority of the Auditorium Theatre Council composed of board members and university administrators, supplemented by civic leaders, the trustees allowed for independence that ultimately resulted in dispute.

For the next four decades the Auditorium Theatre Council sought independence – some said because Council members wanted control of a theater of their own, others that fundraising was easier when donors knew that they were giving directly to the theater, still others that council members wanted dissociation from the proletarian image of the university. In the 1960's, however, the trustees were primarily concerned with resolving a bitter controversy. During the 1970's and '80's separation never really became a question, since the ATC ran deficits and drew upon the university for support – or, to be more specific, upon student tuition. It was not until the late 1980's, when the theater began to profit from a series of enormously popular shows – *Les Miserables*, *Phantom of the Opera*, *Miss Saigon*, and *Show Boat* – that the Council asserted its independence most vigorously.

The issue concerning control of the Auditorium Theatre – whether it was within the jurisdiction of the ATC or Roosevelt University – was sharply drawn when the trustees sought to reallocate $1.5 million

EARLY PROMINENT SPEAKERS AT ROOSEVELT

Dr. Preston Bradley
Pastor, Peoples Church of Chicago
Education and Life
January 1947

Marshall Field
Executive
The American Potential for Greatness
June 1949

Rabbi Jacob J. Weinstein
KAM Temple
The Roosevelt Heritage
January 1950

Walter P. Reuther
President, United Auto Workers,
Trustee, Roosevelt College
Freedom Must Regain the Initiative
January 1951

Leo A. Lerner
Editor and Publisher
Democracy's Challenge to the Educated
June 1951

Percy L. Julian
President, Julian Laboratory
Trustee, Roosevelt University
Science and the Humanities in the 20th Century
January 1955

James P. Warburg
Author
A New Age of Opportunity
June 1957

Niels Bohr
Director of the Institute for Theoretical Physics, Copenhagen, Denmark
Atoms and Human Knowledge
February 1958

W. Averell Harriman
Diplomat
The Summit and the Road Ahead
June 1960

Honorable William O. Douglas
Associate Justice, U.S. Supreme Court
Education for Freedom in the Sixties
January 1963

toward the purchase of the Albert A. Robin Campus in Schaumburg in 1995 and two members of the council responded by suing the University and me. The conclusion to this tale is told in chapter three of this history. But in terms of restoration, governance, and management of the theater, Rolf Weil summarizes the initial relationship well in his memoirs, *Through These Portals:*

> Although Mrs. Spachner should be credited with superhuman fundraising efforts and the restoration of one of the most beautiful theaters in the world, she and her Council developed a desire for independence which made coordination with the University extremely difficult. Although the theater never produced any income for the University's operations and the Council had the benefits of rent-free use of the facilities and of certain auxiliary services from the University, Roosevelt was never appropriately credited. In fact, every effort was made to conceal the affiliation with Roosevelt.

The Auditorium Theatre crisis underscored the precarious financial status of the university. Lerner and his supporters were rightly worried about the priorities of the university. Sparling had the presidential vision to see that the theater could ultimately be an enormous asset to Roosevelt and the larger Chicago community; but given the fiscal constraints of the university at the time, one can imagine why so many withdrew their support of the president. Reconciling the pragmatic and the idealistic approaches proved to be difficult, as Daniel Perlman points out:

> Despite its ultimate resolution, this crisis affected the University more profoundly and for a longer period of time than any other in its history. The issues and events remained poignant for over a decade. One reason for this was that until it was resolved the matter was increasingly a mantle for the issue of who controlled the institution. By the end, it became an open struggle between Sparling and Lerner. Had Lerner not led the the opposition to the establishment of the Auditorium Theatre Council, the faculty and administration dissension might have been resolved internally and not been brought to the Board. But with so eminent a trustee suggesting the president

---

> Genius may be found at any economic or social level. Genius is not a respector of wealth, or ideology, or race.
>
> HON. WILLIAM O. DOUGLAS
> SUPREME COURT JUSTICE
> IN A TALK AT
> ROOSEVELT UNIVERSITY

Playful Times

A time for the hokey-pokey, a festive opera or a Grant Park scrimmage, Roosevelt students made the most of their "break" from studies and classes.

Dedicated to the Enlightenment of the Human Spirit

Students could expect an active social life on campus. Both university and student-sponsored events were popular and well-attended.

Central photo:

In June of 1956, graduates and guests enjoyed the talents of a singer and band at the annual Final Fling Dance held at Covenant Club.

Pictured below from left:

The hot dance number at the 1957 Christmas dance was one guaranteed to put a smile on students' faces – "The Hokey-Pokey."

Members of the Roosevelt College Opera Workshop hoist tankards and raise their voices during the January 1954 rehearsal of "Cavalleria Rusticana." Lois Raye (seated) played Lola, the carefree flirt whose actions bring on the tragedy in Pietro Mascagni's account of Sicilian village life.

October is football weather and time for Coach Edwin Turner (center, in jacket) to get the 1964 intramural team warmed up on the frosty fields of Grant Park.

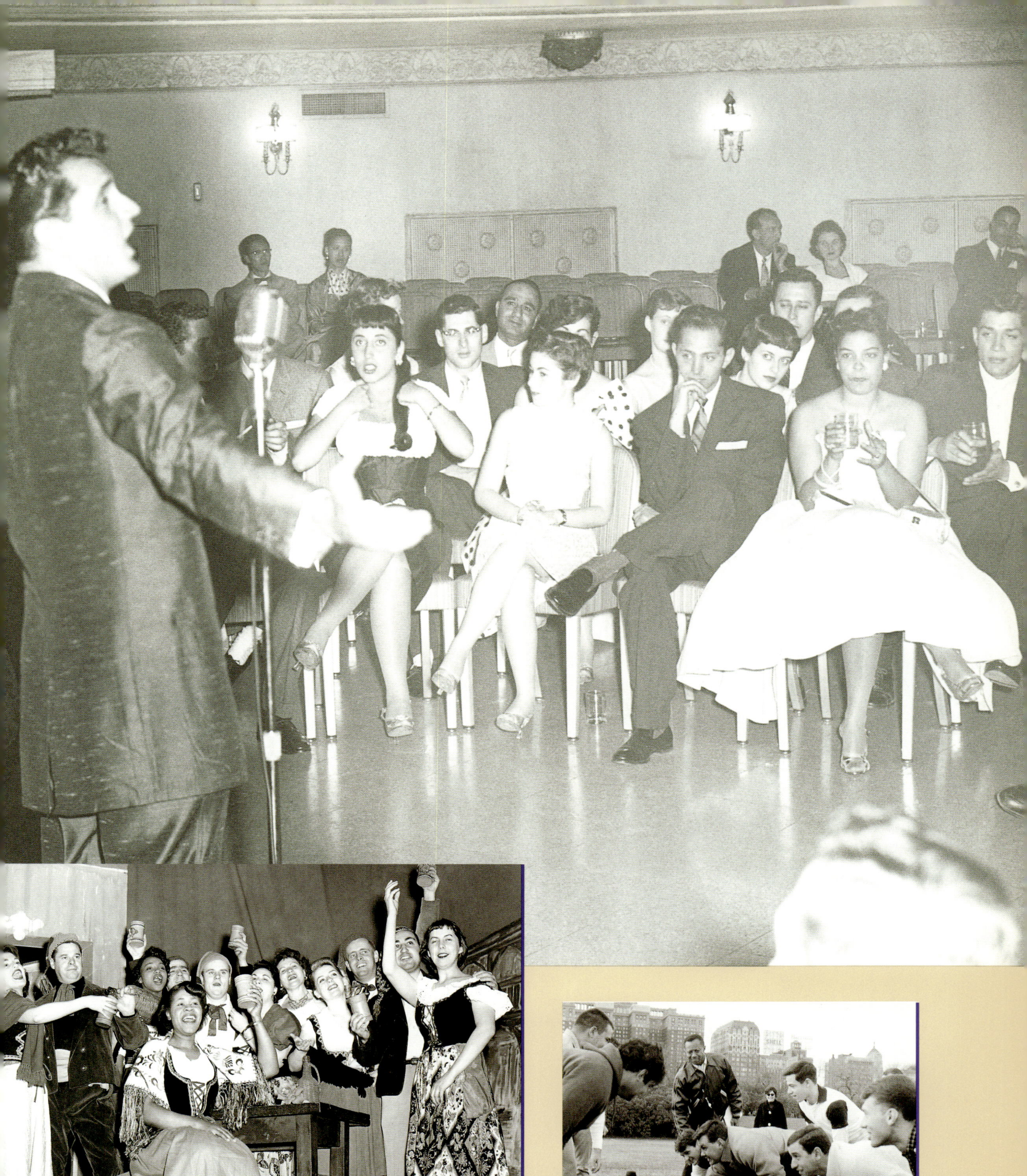

was mistaken, the position of the dissidents within the institution was sanctioned.

Sparling was the victor, and ultimately his long-range vision would be affirmed, but the authority of his presidency was severely eroded. Sparling himself considered the battle a Pyrrhic victory and ultimately a defeat. Few academic leaders would have had the courage and determination to found a university like Roosevelt or imagine the possibilities of an Auditorium Theatre. Sparling had triumphed in the Auditorium Theatre crisis, as he had in breaking away from the Central YMCA College and in creating the new institution itself, but he had lost credibility with some board members and administrative leaders. By the early 1960's, there was a need for fiscal stability and predictability, and a long overdue invitation to the business community to share in a partnership essential to any enduring success.

The university had been in debt for all but one year of its history. From 1962 to 1965, the budget deficits were acute, and now the president found himself in a tense relationship with Harland Allen, the chairman who succeeded Leo Lerner. He threatened retirement on several occasions and when he did so during a particularly difficult meeting, Allen took him up on his statement immediately so that Sparling could not withdraw. The chairman moved swiftly to set up a search committee for the second president of the university and the transition began. Sparling would live until 1981 and could look back upon a university created and developed out of his original vision of equal opportunity to students of all backgrounds. A vision of Jefferson's "natural aristocracy." Of Emerson's "pragmatic idealism." Of Dewey's "democracy in education." It was a remarkable achievement. It was indeed a noble vision.

1959 Eleanor Roosevelt (far right) came to the university eight times to attend important functions. One of those occasions was the Diamond Jubilee dinner. Joining her on the dais were Mrs. Sparling, Mrs. Richard Daley, Mayor Richard Daley, and President Sparling.

The appointment of a new president is the most important task that confronts a board of trustees, and it is always filled with anxiety for any university community. In the case of Roosevelt, the transition was particularly difficult, for the university was almost insolvent fiscally. Sparling had defined a magnificent mission for Roosevelt University and implemented it with the gusto of a charismatic leader. But by the 1960's – in the aftermath of the acquisition of CMC, the Auditorium Theatre crisis, and persistent deficits – the university needed managerial and fiscal stability. On the one hand, Roosevelt would be entering one of the most tempestuous decades of the century, with uprisings from ethnic groups, women, and students; at the same time, a two-year branch of the University of Illinois would transform itself into the four-year "Circle Campus," later the University of Illinois at Chicago, and threaten enrollments. Regrettably, Roosevelt had not yet made a serious effort to create credibility with the business community.

Unfortunately, the search for a president to follow the university's forceful founder resulted in a mistaken choice that made the year 1964 particularly painful and left Roosevelt in an even more perilous state. The tenure of the second president, Robert Pitchell, lasted for only twelve months in 1964. Appointed on October 24, 1963, Pitchell assumed office on January 1, 1964, and was asked to resign as of December 31, 1964. A forty-two year old political scientist trained at Fordham and the University of California, he had been director of the Institute of Public Administration at Indiana University and an administrative assistant to Senator Birch Bayh.

Pitchell seemed a sensible choice as the successor to Sparling, for he was a political liberal who combined scholarship and action. But he was accustomed to the traditional administration of a state university and was troubled by Roosevelt's democratic culture and the extremity of its shared governance. According to Rolf Weil, who served as secretary to the presidential search committee and was dean of business administration at the time, there was a

1964 Robert Pitchell (left) is Roosevelt's forgotten president. Shown here with Elliott Roosevelt, Pitchell, the former director of public administration at Indiana University, only served as president for one year because he lost the support of his deans and the Board of Trustees.

"Board-commissioned study conducted by Cresap, McCormick and Paget [that] recommended removal of faculty from the Board, the abolishing of votes of confidence, and the discontinuation of the faculty budget committee. Unfortunately, Pitchell did not have the diplomatic skills necessary to bring about smooth change. Fears created by these recommendations and the disaffection on the part of the deans soon made it almost impossible for Pitchell to function." Although there was deep financial need, there was also strong pride which was highly critical of certain efforts to change the institutional image in ways which might have made it more attractive to donors. When Pitchell sought to centralize authority in his office, there was rebellion by top administrators who were accustomed to participate in all decisions.

The administrative rebellion was close to a coup d'etat and was branded by students as "the revolt of the deans," although Frank Untermyer, a professor of political science at the time, remembers that the "'revolt,' if any, was by President Pitchell, and against his own deans. Those who can recall the stormy and unhappy year of Pitchell's incumbency will recall his constant, annoyed rebukes of Otto Wirth, frequently in public situations."

The deans resisted Pitchell's attempt to make governance of the university more traditional, to give order and discipline to an administration that they agreed lacked system and organization. After Pitchell fired an able vice president for business and finance and instituted what were considered (by Roosevelt standards) inappropriate expenditures for his office, the deans demanded action by the board. The trustees then directed Pitchell to be responsible for exclusively external affairs, especially fundraising, and the council of deans for internal, academic matters; in the case of any disagreement between the president and the deans, they reasoned, the board of trustees would be the arbiter. Of course, this was an impossibly irregular administrative structure, for it undermined the president's authority entirely.

Lyle Spencer

One dean was so upset with Pitchell that he sent a psychological profile to the Chairman of the Board, Lyle Spencer, describing the president's lack of fitness for the position; other deans threatened to resign. The conflict between the deans and the president inevitably was shared by the faculty and then the students until Pitchell could no longer function effectively as president.

Weil, who was the elected chairman of the administrative council, found himself a central figure in the confused administrative structure that Lyle Spencer and the trustees established. Spencer himself struggled to keep order in the university. He had been brought on the board by Sparling as a promising young entrepreneur from the University of Chicago and later established Science Research Associates, which administered the census for the government of Japan. Spencer joined the Board of Directors of IBM, which had bought S.R.A. for millions of dollars. He died at an early age, unfortunately leaving little to Roosevelt University; instead, he established the Spencer Foundation, which is devoted to educational research. During his chairmanship, from 1964 to 1968, Spencer grew to depend increasingly on Rolf Weil.

1961 While these students enjoyed an idyllic moment in Grant Park, the Sparling administration was facing budget deficits, problems with the Auditorium Theatre and a leveling off of enrollments.

Although Lyle Spencer wanted to avoid any public revelations of internal difficulties, the *Chicago Tribune* reported that the *Torch*, the student newspaper, had "carried a 'bulletin' [on November 14] saying that Pitchell had been 'unofficially fired,' that he 'now has no administrative power,' that the university was in debt, and 'may cease to exist within the next two years.'" Some unidentified source had leaked the deliberations of the deans, and though rather apocalyptic in its colorful phrasing, the account in the *Torch* was not far from the truth.

Pitchell and Spencer vehemently denied the story. The student newspaper was impounded but nevertheless found wide circulation; the five student editors were dismissed from the staff, and then appealed to the A.C.L.U. There were threats of resignations from other administrators and the faculty, staff, and students were in a state of administrative paralysis. Finally, Pitchell sent a letter to Spencer in which he said that "I no longer see the possibility of success in carrying out my present responsibilities beyond the current term of appointment."

Lyle Spencer asked Rolf Weil to be Acting President, with the understanding that he would not be a candidate for the presidency. As Weil remembered these events, his "marching orders from the board were clear: restore the fiscal integrity of the University, improve its image, and create stability – a tall order indeed." The accumulated deficit was $800,000 and the annual budget $4.8 million; Weil had to "negotiate a line of credit at the American National Bank in order to meet the payroll punctually."

Meanwhile, the University of Illinois made it clear that a second campus of major proportions would be established in Chicago. Two former Teachers Colleges – Northeastern Illinois University and Chicago State University – were directly competitive, attracting the same type of students at one-fourth the tuition of Roosevelt. In the suburbs, other public institutions, Northern Illinois and Governors State, were drawing students who might have come to the university. At the same time, the two major Catholic universities, Loyola and DePaul, were becoming

The Auditorium Building, Roosevelt University's signature structure, is magnificent in every season.

more diverse in their student body, ecumenical in their curriculum, and increasingly competitive. Social justice, equal educational opportunity, affirmative action, diversity – all of the shibboleths of Roosevelt University in the forties and fifties were now the currency of these other institutions. Roosevelt would retain its original mission but now had to adapt itself to the changing city and growing suburbs. It had to reach out to the corporate community. It had to become more of a traditional university.

    A tall order, indeed.

> Whatever raises the standard of life in any part of the world or among any group of people raises it among all.
>
> ALBEN BARKLEY
> VICE PRESIDENT OF THE UNITED STATES,
> IN A TALK AT ROOSEVELT UNIVERSITY

Consolidation

ROLF A. WEIL

The three primary presidents of Roosevelt University have been well matched for each of its seasons. Sparling was a fearless idealist who founded the university in the spirit of social justice and struggled to establish a foundation for the future. Weil was a pragmatist who instituted fiscal integrity and managed the university effectively during three decades of student turbulence and growing competition. And I reversed declining enrollments and sought to marry the vision of Sparling with the pragmatism of Weil into a metropolitan vision for the twenty-first century. The university has been fortunate indeed to discover the right leader for each of its three seasons.

The president who provided continuity between past and present, the man who embodied so many of the characteristics of the university – upward mobility, idealistic fervor, high academic standards, and practicality – was Rolf Weil. No one still active at Roosevelt has been there longer, and his influence was profound. Weil's leadership of the Business College during the Sparling years, his influence on fellow deans during the precarious Pitchell interregnum, and his 24-year administration, from 1965 to 1988, defined Roosevelt University in the eyes of most Chicagoans.

Rolf Weil came to America as a refugee from Nazi Germany in the 1930's. The subtitle of his memoirs, *Through These Portals*, suggests the remarkable journey he traveled: "From Immigrant to University President." He was awarded his PhD in economics from the University of Chicago and began teaching at Roosevelt in 1946, advancing swiftly to become Dean of the Business College, then acting president in 1965 when the university was foundering, and president in 1966. Becoming a university president was for Rolf Weil the realization of the American dream. As he writes in his memoirs: "Only in America, it seems to me, is it possible for an immigrant with a minority group background and without substantial financial resources to be rewarded this way."

1965 Rolf Weil was 44 years old when he became Roosevelt's acting president. His charge was to restore the fiscal integrity of the university, improve its image and create stability.

Arthur Hillman and Wayne Leys

David Kleinerman

1964 Don Kirschner (with hat) nominated as "Top Prof" is introduced by Paul Johnson.

Weil had several characteristics that were particularly important for leadership in the sixties, when the university was buffeted by internal chaos, which he could correct, and a series of external revolutions beyond his or anyone's control. He was a man of absolute integrity; he was conservative fiscally and academically; and he was a realist who confronted each difficult situation as it arose on its own terms. An immigrant who was now a university president, he never took for granted the gift of America. He balanced the books of his university, and he negotiated with students who demanded racial, student, and gender equality and decried a war they thought was unjustified; but through it all, Rolf Weil never lost his gratitude to the country that had given him an education, a family, and a career. He was indeed a man who matched the needs of Roosevelt University in the 1960's.

The most pressing need was to balance the budget. The university had been in deficit for all but one of its twenty years, which created great instability internally and difficulties in seeking funds from individual and corporate donors. Weil assembled a remarkable group of administrators to help him impose discipline on a university that had no endowment and was therefore completely dependent on tuition, an institution in an Auditorium Building that had suffered from decades of deferred maintenance and that had not yet raised any significant funds in the corporate community of Chicago.

Weil appointed his good friend, Otto Wirth, as vice president for academic affairs. Wirth was a fellow immigrant from Germany who also believed deeply in the utopian mission of the university and as someone who enjoyed the respect of the faculty and was a distinguished scholar of German culture, he brought stature to his position.

David Kleinerman became controller during the early years of Weil's presidency; he had also risen from the ranks of the faculty and not only possessed a strong background in accounting and a keen understanding of the fiscal dilemmas the university

1965 Roosevelt University's brightest students competed in the national College Bowl on NBC-TV in New York. Roosevelt lost to the eventual champions from Baldwin-Wallace College, 250 to 200.

Lawrence Silverman

Daniel Perlman

Wendell Arnold

Harold Bland

confronted but had a sensitivity to the faculty and staff. Kleinerman would return to the faculty and then, in the 1980's, serve for a year as acting dean of the Business College. Kleinerman was replaced by Harold Bland. He served faithfully through the first year of my administration in 1989, then became a member of the business faculty.

Lawrence Silverman was vice president for student services and, as someone who lived in Glenview, was particularly aware of the migration of the middle class from Chicago, a city burdened by a faltering public school system and racially segregated neighborhoods, to the suburbs. He became the champion of Roosevelt's presence in the area northwest of Chicago and sowed the seeds for a direction that would become crucial during a period when institutions like the University of Illinois at Chicago, Loyola, DePaul, and Northeastern were becoming increasingly competitive within the city.

Daniel Perlman served as assistant to the president and then vice president for administrative services. Beyond his normal duties, he turned his attention to the governance of the university, the restoration of the Auditorium Building, and the development of numerous government grants. Perlman was a gifted administrator whose lengthy document on governance, published in 1971, was the most important and complete account of the university until that time; he went on to become president of Suffolk and Webster Universities.

The vice president for development was Wendell Arnold, a man of great common sense and creativity who came to Roosevelt University in 1967 and devoted himself to organizing, for the first time in the history of the institution, a development office that would professionalize fundraising.

Before Rolf Weil could stabilize his administration and attend to the more traditional tasks of the university – recruitment, the development of curriculum, the promotion of research, the acquisition of external funds, and the creation of an endowment – colleges and universities were struck by the greatest student revolution in American history, and Roosevelt was not spared. Indeed, the civil rights movement that had emerged in the early part of the decade simply confirmed the creation of Roosevelt University twenty years earlier. Student resistance to all forms of authority found a responsive chord here.

Relations between students and administrative officials heated up in 1967, when the Roosevelt community supported the efforts of Martin Luther King and his followers in civil rights demonstrations and nationwide protests against the Vietnam War. Together with faculty and administrators, students took issue with the federal government's policy of "ranking" them, which exempted from military service those in the upper half of their class and caused minorities and the poor to be drafted in disproportionately higher numbers. As part of their dissension, radical students pressed the administration to allow the university to become an official haven. Weil resisted and established a policy that permitted protest without the disruption of university operations, but he was accused of being too moderate.

1967 The Auditorium Theatre's $3-million restoration project, headed by Chicago architect Harry Weese, finally was complete and the theatre reopened with the New York City Ballet performing *A Midsummer Night's Dream*.

1978 Beatrice Spachner, chairman of the Auditorium Theatre Council, accepts the David C. Finley Award from James Biddle, president of the National Trust for Historic Preservation, for restoration of the Auditorium Building and the Auditorium Theatre.

The Board of Trustees, as Jerome Stone (a trustee since 1954 and Chairman of the Board from 1968 to 1983) remembers, was not only important but impressive in those days. "I remember getting calls from parents of students saying that we were condemning them to death in Vietnam if we expelled them from the school. Rolf and I had many conversations about how to react to the public. But it was his firm stand backed by the Board which was practical and within the bounds of university regulations that stood the day; and for the first time we received accolades from the press and the business community, and I think as the problems went on, the whole community as well."

The number of extremists was small in comparison to many other universities and the effect of student unrest on Roosevelt in the long term was minimal, but at the time it was a site of demonstrations, highlighted by those of the 1968 Democratic Convention held across the street in Grant Park and farther south along Michigan Avenue, at the Hilton Hotel.

The national phenomenon of student violence against administrative authority had spread from Columbia University and The City College of New York [CCNY] in the east to the University of Wisconsin in the midwest, and the University of California at Berkeley and Stanford in the west. The concerns about racial and gender discrimination were triggered to a great extent by those students who were threatened to be drafted into a Vietnam War they regarded as misguided. Ethnic studies departments were created at many universities; traditional curricula were severely modified to accommodate minority groups that had been historically underrepresented; open admissions burst forth at institutions like CCNY, which had been highly selective and now embraced far more underprepared students. In this environment, Roosevelt suffered less than most other institutions, for it had always been known for its inclusiveness and had adopted educational programs for the culturally deprived as a matter of course. Still, the university could not escape the academic turmoil and the social transformations that pervaded the nation. Its confrontation between students, faculty and administration reflected the national mood and then, as if in search of a martyr, it focused upon the application of one Staughton Lynd who sought full-time appointment to the faculty.

Lynd was an outspoken opponent of the Vietnam War. He had been denied tenure at Yale University as well as appointments at Chicago State University and the University of Chicago.

1964 Rudolph Ganz, a world-renowned composer, conductor and pianist, celebrated the 100th anniversary of the Chicago Musical College with graduating students. CMC, which had merged with Roosevelt in 1954, was a financial drain for many years, but its talented faculty and students have contributed much to both Roosevelt's and Chicago's cultural life.

1966 Rudolph Ganz, Music Dean Joseph Creanza and pianist Arthur Rubenstein shared stories at a luncheon.

Turmoil

Not spared the turmoil that rocked campuses across the country in the late '60's, President Weil was required clearly to define the limits of protest.

In the 1960's, issues ranging from the Vietnam War to the failure of a controversal candidate to win faculty appointment resulted in pressure techniques and threats against the administration which in turn led to sit-ins and other forms of protest. Despite the turmoil, Roosevelt never shut down.

Against this backdrop, President Rolf Weil issued Roosevelt University's "Statement on Freedom of Expression" on November 16, 1967, which stated in part: "The era of the 1960's can best be characterized as one of ferment. Throughout our nation answers are being sought to new and complex questions regarding political, social or ethical principles. By its very nature, the modern university has become one of the major wellsprings of action which focuses on the search for answers to these questions.

"For this quest of knowledge to continue it is necessary that all members of the university community be assured that their freedoms of speech and inquiry not be abrogated by the actions of others within this community....It may be superfluous to remind all that in its short but vivid history Roosevelt University has supported and will continue to support these basic concepts of freedom."

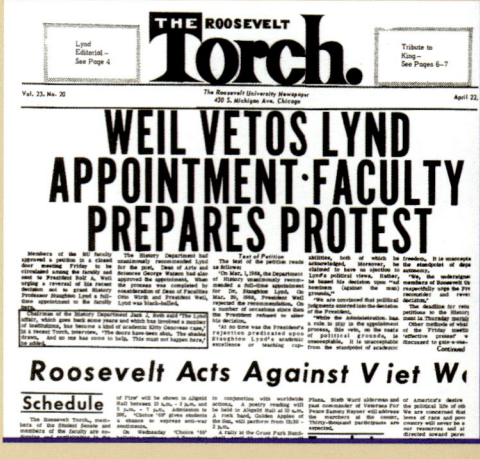

58

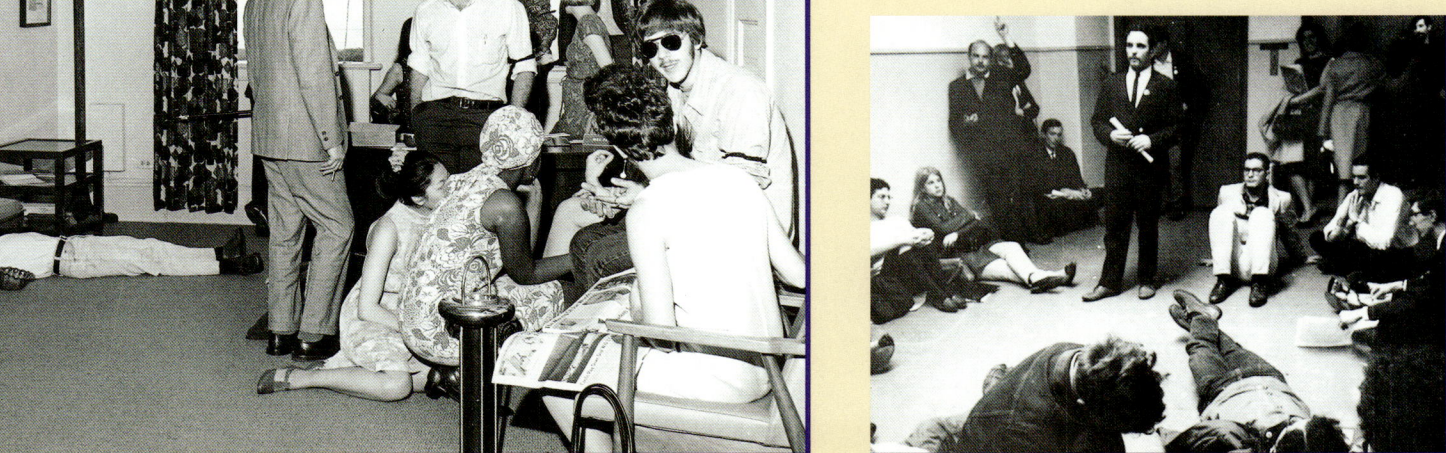

He became a part-time instructor at Roosevelt and then applied for a three-year contract that he hoped would begin in September 1968. He was recommended by faculty committees and the Dean of the College of Arts and Sciences. The Dean of Faculties, who was the principal academic officer of the university, and the President overruled them on *ad hominem* grounds, asserting that Lynd's contentious personality would be dysfunctional in the university at large. Weil had always been a champion of academic freedom and of course had known discrimination in Nazi Germany first-hand so that he was particularly sensitive to freedom of expression. He proclaimed the right of dissenters to voice whatever objections they wished so long as they did not disrupt the operations of the university; but he also asserted his authority as president to make the ultimate judgment on personnel. He stood firm on his decision not to offer Staughton Lynd a three-year contract.

In retrospect, the Lynd case seems a manifestation of the times and disproportionate to the overall governance of the university, for it involved only an initial full-time appointment that was not even on a tenure track. Indeed, it seems surprising that Weil had to defend his action at all – but the temper of the times and the outcry of internal and external forces demanded a public statement by the president. Lynd became a lightning rod for the Roosevelt community, embodying the tensions of protest and authority that raged throughout the sixties; his case not only polarized some students and faculty against the administration but attracted community activists who used it for their own political and public purposes. The issue attracted the mainstream press, and sides were firmly drawn – some defending Weil as having the ultimate authority of the president to appoint anyone he wished, others claiming that the democratic spirit of Roosevelt was being betrayed by not allowing a controversial champion of social justice to find a place in the very university that mirrored Lynd's values.

Chicago's American, Wednesday, February 19, 1969

Roosevelt Prexy Speaks

Protests Justifiable— to a Point, Says Weil

BY PAT DALTON

Dr. Rolf A. Weil, president of Roosevelt university, is a man who knows a lot about student rebellions, both first-hand and academically.

He has been studying student outbursts since the first one began at the University of California in Berkeley in 1964. During the last week, he has been dealing with black student protesters on his own campus who claim the study program for blacks is inadequate.

There were no demonstrations at Roosevelt yesterday. A student faculty committee met last night and agreed on a plan to establish a black studies department.

The plan was formed by the Black Studies Curriculum committee. It calls for the Black Student association to draft a specific course of study and administrative operation.

It would have to be approved by the curriculum committee of the undergraduate division, and then by the full faculty of that division.

Blacks Halt Protests

A B.S.A. spokesman said demonstrations would be suspended until the faculty votes on the proposal. The B.S.A. will hold a meeting tomorrow to work on the matter.

Weil thinks these campus explosions can be harnessed and "will reach a peak and decline this year if college administrators take a firm stand."

If the administrators don't do this, he fears that "radical, military groups such as the New Left may be counteracted by the formation of a New Right that will create more white racism than we have ever known."

"Students have justifiable grievances, and sometimes we take them too lightly," Weil said in a speech Wednesday at the Sherman House during the 64th anniversary meeting of the Rotary Club of Chicago. "We must find out what it is they want and what we can do about it.

"But we can't permit students to disrupt the very education that might be able to solve the problems that brought on the protests, such as war and racism."

Promises Harsh Discipline

Weil said, "If I have one job to do, it is to provide freedom to learn for those who want to learn, and freedom to teach for those who want to teach. I will use whatever discipline is needed—whether from the university or thru civil and criminal charges—to inforce this freedom.

"It is our responsibility to see to it that we use the funds given to us by taxpayers or from tuitions for the purpose for which the money was given to us."

Weil said, "There is a place for civil disobedience to call attention to wrongs by those who are willing to pay the price. There is a place for a hunger strike by a Ghandi, who was willing to die, or for demonstrations by a Martin Luther King, who was willing to go to jail.

"But these students break a law and then scream, 'Amnesty.'"

Ordinarily, the case would have been no more than the usual academic squabble concerning personnel in which faculty committees and the central administration differ – with the president almost invariably prevailing. Its importance in the history of Roosevelt University is that democratic governance was tested publicly. Roosevelt could no longer function as a maverick university where the term "shared governance" had been more literally applied than in almost any other institution. From the origins of the university, faculty had served on the budget and other critical committees; there were votes of confidence in administrators, which limited their ability to take unpopular positions; and students actively participated in decision making. These were the characteristics of a democratic institution, but they had led to a lack of clarity in administration and surely they impeded action. Roosevelt had to mature like other institutions, developing shared governance in more traditional terms. Faculty would control curriculum, administration supervise management, and students concern themselves with coursework.

Amid personal attacks by some students and faculty, Rolf Weil maintained his consistent position. At one point, a liberal rabbi drew a three-minute ovation from a crowd of sympathizers when he claimed that "we have reached the point where we must say that either Lynd is allowed to teach at Roosevelt or there will be no Roosevelt University." A noted historian from Northwestern, Christopher Lasch, who himself had taught at Roosevelt University and was leader of the Committee on Academic Freedom, announced a possible boycott and proposed to censure the university because Weil's veto of Lynd's appointment was a "breach of academic freedom" and an invasion of faculty rights. The American Association of University Professors considered a formal censure of the university. Studs Terkel publicly condemned Roosevelt and refused to speak there (a threat he later recanted). An African-American entertainer, Oscar Brown Jr., would not accept an alumni award because Lynd's rejection ran

1976 Professors St. Clair Drake, sociology, and Frank Untermyer, political science, were faculty leaders who, in 1960, taught together in Ghana and Tanzania.

1974 Roosevelt students meet in a Black Film Workshop. During the turbulent 1960's, black students pressed the administration to create a Black Studies Curriculum.

Staughton Lynd

CHICAGO SUN-TIMES

The University Destroyers

A group of outside professors and other agitators have threatened to destroy Roosevelt University unless it hires the controversial history professor, Staughton Lynd. They say they are acting in the cause of academic freedom but surely the principle of academic freedom does not encompass the destruction of the temple in which the freedom must be practiced.

The group of outside professors, including one from Northwestern University and one from Northern Illinois University, said that it would urge teachers to refuse to accept jobs at Roosevelt unless Lynd was given a full-time appointment. One other member of the group said, "Either Lynd will be teaching at Roosevelt University or there will be no more Roosevelt University."

This outrageous threat calls for a counterattack by friends and alumni of Roosevelt University and, we should hope, by the faculty of Roosevelt itself who know better than anyone else the long record of respect for academic freedom built by Roosevelt University.

Lynd's case has been magnified out of all proportion to its importance. He was recommended for a permanent appointment by the Roosevelt history faculty. The appointment was vetoed by President Rolf A. Weil on the ground that Lynd's personality did not suit him to be permanently employed. Lynd is presently a part-time faculty member.

Lynd first came to the attention of the public when he made an unauthorized trip to Vietnam in 1965. His supporters jump to the conclusion that Lynd's rejection by Weil is based on the leftist professor's political beliefs. This violates the principle of academic constitution of Roosevelt University specifically states that when a candidate is turned down for a post no reasons need be given.

It doesn't take much research to find reasons why President Weil would find Lynd an unsuitable personality for the university. At Yale, Lynd was turned down for permanent tenure long before he became involved in the controversy over Vietnam. Yale officials have an opinion about his personality.

A clue about Lynd's personality is in a quotation from him that appeared in Charles Bartlett's column in The Sun-Times May 8. Lynd advocated "occupying" university offices until policy-makers "enter into a dialog with us and mankind." He is advocating what students have been doing in various schools although such action is condemned by officials of the American Assn. of University Professors.

Some of the outside professors who say they will destroy Roosevelt unless Lynd is appointed say they are leaders in the Illinois chapter of the American Assn. of University Professors. They should be condemning the actions of the students who disrupted operations at Roosevelt instead of encouraging continued student revolt.

It is our understanding that the minority of students who have been demonstrating for Lynd were ready to settle for compromises offered by President Weil—but not including capitulation on Lynd—when haranguing by the outsiders prevented a settlement. As Weil said, for the outsiders to come in while the university was trying to work out an agreement with the dissenting students was like shouting "fire" in a crowded theater.

"contrary to the principles of academic and personal freedom for which Roosevelt publicly and proudly stood when I was a student there." The "Students for Quality Education" made demands upon the administration which were answered, if not fully satisfied. Eighty-six members of the faculty protested Weil's refusal to give reasons why he would not appoint Lynd – he had simply said that the political activist was "publicity prone" and that his decision was *ad hominem* or personal. The Lynd affair became a crisis between a faculty asserting academic freedom – no one questioned Lynd's abilities as a scholar or a teacher – and a president exercising his authority on behalf of the entire institution, claiming the candidate would be dysfunctional if appointed.

The pressures from community leaders, faculty, administrators, and alumni were reflections of the tempestuous times, and they tested Weil's resolve. The statement of the history department accused "the Roosevelt Administration" of consistently "claiming to be in favor of academic freedom (although it is qualified by asserting that such freedom begins with tenure)," but "its position in the Lynd case has illustrated the opposite." An editorial in *The Chicago Tribune* of May 13, 1968, supported the president and his board of trustees:

A President's Duty

President Rolf A. Weil of Roosevelt University continues resolute in refusing to abdicate the responsibilities of his office. Those include approval or disapproval of faculty appointments and use when needful of such sanctions as suspension and expulsion in defense of order and respect for regulation....

Staughton Lynd, the "new left" historian whose status at Roosevelt University is the occasion of current controversy there, argues that student participation in coercive sit-ins there should be immune from disciplinary action and from trespass charges. That fact alone provides a simple confirmation of President Weil's judgment not to appoint him to the Roosevelt full time faculty. Student and faculty voices may and should be heard by administrators – in civil terms and thru appropriate

1967 At a party sponsored by Friends and Fellows of Roosevelt University, (from left) Elmer Gertz, Percy Julian, Rolf Weil and Morris Bialis discuss activities at the university.

1970 Among those attending Roosevelt University's 25th anniversary party were trustees Leo Lerner and Eric Kohler.

channels. But in academic government executive responsibility must and therefore should be in the hands of the chief executive. President Weil is demonstrating what should be obvious to all.

It was not accidental that Weil received an honorary degree from Loyola University in Chicago (which also denied Lynd an appointment) for his "courageous" stand in the defense of academic freedom during the period of student unrest in the late 1960's.

Another manifestation of student protest was the demand for a program in black studies – a movement that was prevalent throughout higher education in the late sixties and seventies, and an inevitable academic outgrowth of the civil rights movement. Encouraged by national organizations like the Black Panthers, students submitted "non-negotiable demands" for courses in Swahili, black history, literature, and other subjects that focused upon their heritage. At one point 150 students occupied Weil's office, calling for "black studies or no studies," threatening him so personally that he required police protection for several days and had to transfer his office to the basement of the Congress Hotel. Weil's position again was consistent and clear, as quoted by the press:

> Weil thinks these campus explosions can be harnessed and "will reach a peak and decline this year if college administrators take a firm stand."
>
> If the administrators don't do this, he fears that "radical, militant groups such as the new Left may be counteracted by the formation of a New Right that will create more white racism than we have ever known."
>
> "Students have justifiable grievances, and sometimes we take them too lightly," Weil said in a speech Wednesday at the Sherman House during the 64th anniversary meeting of the Rotary Club of Chicago. "We must find out what it is they want and what we can do about it.
>
> "But we can't permit students to disrupt the very education that might be able to solve the problems that brought on the protests, such as war and racism."
>
> Weil said, "If I have one job to do, it is to provide

Team Spirit

At Roosevelt University, the recreational needs of students were not neglected although the emphasis was always upon scholarship.

Sporting activities at Roosevelt were popular in the 1960's, 1970's and early '80's. The university had teams in basketball, soccer, intramural football, golf and tennis.

Central photo:

The Roosevelt University Lakers basketball team of 1977-78 was invited to play a few games in Central America.

Pictured below from left:

Roosevelt and McKendree College players go for the ball during a soccer match in 1985.

A Laker on the 1986-87 team left his opponents flat footed.

The 1989 soccer team had a season of 7 wins, 1 tie and 4 losses.

Dedicated to the Enlightenment of the Human Spirit

> Unless a free press and a free people reside here, in this great, generous and capacious land, they will reside nowhere on this minor planet.
>
> EDWARD R. MURROW
> NEWSCASTER,
> IN A TALK AT ROOSEVELT UNIVERSITY

freedom to learn for those who want to learn, and freedom to teach for those who want to teach. I will use whatever discipline is needed – whether from the university or thru civil and criminal charges – to enforce this freedom.

"It is our responsibility to see to it that we use the funds given to us by taxpayers or from tuitions for the purpose for which the money was given to us."

Weil said there is a place for civil disobedience to call attention to wrongs by those who are willing to pay the price. There is a place for a hunger strike by a Ghandi, who was willing to die, or for demonstrations by a Martin Luther King, who was willing to go to jail.

"But these students break a law and then scream, 'Amnesty.'"

The number of militant students at Roosevelt was really quite small and their protest an echo of the national movement for a greater presence of African-American culture in higher education. In New York, Los Angeles, and other cities, this movement led to ethnic studies departments that have now made African-American culture a separate course of study in the curriculum. Paradoxically, Roosevelt had been a pioneer in this effort and had appointed distinguished black intellectuals to the faculty from its inception: St. Clair Drake, the sociologist; Lorenzo Turner, the linguist; Charles Hamilton, the political scientist, and others.

As early as 1946, Otto Wirth had established a department of culture studies "to reduce intercultural fear and suspicion" and, together with Frank Untermyer and other white faculty, had reinforced Sparling's desire to include African-Americans as a vital force in the Roosevelt community. The militants of the '60's were few in number and their protest small in comparison to the large number of black students – approximately 28% of the student body at the time – who, like their white counterparts, were non-ideological; they pursued a traditional education that they hoped would lead to productive careers. Still, there was some truth in the protests that Roosevelt did not have enough black administrators and faculty, even though the pool of black applicants was relatively small. It would take many years before the university truly made overt efforts to have a significant proportion of African-Americans in leadership roles within the administration, the faculty and board of trustees; and even today the number of minorities, including now Hispanics, Asians, and women is insufficient.

As someone trained in economics and conservative by nature, Rolf Weil was naturally prepared to set the finances of the university in order. He was fortunate to have an administration, faculty, and staff that understood the necessary reforms and budget restraints. Their salaries were low and their workload heavy. Looking back upon the university community of this period a half century later, one must be impressed by the idealism, generosity and cooperation of what was truly a Roosevelt University family – they seem like the characteristics of a bygone era. Of course there was a price to pay. As Weil notes in his autobiography:

At Roosevelt University the combination of triennial votes of confidence (abandoned in my last year in office), faculty involvement in budget decisions and faculty representation on the Board of Trustees as well as the tradition of academic democracy necessitated great diplomacy in creating any change especially in the academic sphere. Politics exists in all organizations but I believe that it has reached the highest levels of sophistication in the academic community. During my twenty-four years in the president's office I learned to live with both the formal and informal political structure of the institution. But I must admit that at times it was exasperating to have to move much more slowly and carefully to bring about change than was warranted by the need for adaptation to new conditions.

As Weil began his presidency, it became clear that the university could no longer depend exclusively on student tuition and a few scattered gifts from wealthy donors. The time had come for a more formal approach to fundraising and a more activist relationship with the philanthropic community of Chicago.

1981 Jerome H. Stone (left), photographed with President Weil in Roosevelt's lobby, is one of the university's most influential trustees. A former CEO of Stone Container Corporation, Stone joined the board in 1953 and was chairman from 1969 until 1983.

1968 Trustee Jerome Stone, Mayor Richard J. Daley and President Weil attended groundbreaking ceremonies for Roosevelt's residence hall, the Herman Crown Center. It was made possible by a gift from the Crown family and a federal construction loan.

1971 The Herman Crown Center (the 17-story building on the left) is adjacent to the Auditorium Building at 425 S. Wabash Avenue. It has rooms for 300 students and also features a student union, cafeteria, computer classroom, and center for academic assistance. The center cost $4.8 million to build.

The key figure in the development of professional fundraising was Jerome Stone, one of the great civic leaders in Chicago during the past fifty years and a critical figure in the modern history of Roosevelt University. Stone was a member of the family that had built the Stone Container Corporation and became its president and COO in 1972, and its chairman and CEO in 1975. A highly successful and disciplined business executive, he knew the corporate community well and began to make connections for the university by building the board of trustees and laying the foundation for fundraising. Beyond his business acumen and friendships with other leaders, Stone was a cultivated man who was deeply involved in a whole range of civic enterprises. At various times, he was an important leader in the organization of the Economic Development Commission and similar projects: the creation of a temple for the North Shore Congregation Israel in Glencoe, development of the Chicago Public Library, the formation of the National Organization for Alzheimers Disease and Related Disorders and, later in his philanthropic career, the deputy chairman of the Museum of Contemporary Art. In higher education his loyalty was always to Roosevelt. He became a board member in 1953 and was elected as chairman from 1967 to 1983. Since then he has remained active as chairman emeritus.

During the tenure of Rolf Weil and Jerome Stone, many projects were realized. One of the most important was the construction of the Herman Crown Center, a facility made possible in 1970 by the Crown family and a federal construction loan. Although Roosevelt had always been and would remain primarily a commuter campus, there was a call for a student union and a residence hall adjacent to the Auditorium Building that would allow students to go directly from their living quarters to classrooms without walking outside. The dormitory would also create a stable, residential community that had not existed previously. The Crown Center housed approximately 300 students. Initially, it was

From Top:

1970 Thanks to a $2 million gift from the Walter E. Heller Foundation and support from the Higher Education Facilities Act, Roosevelt constructed a 10-story classroom, laboratory and library facility in what had been a light and air court in the center of the Auditorium Building. Looking at the construction plans were President Weil, trustee Alyce DeCosta and architect Harry Weese.

1973 Alyce DeCosta was obviously pleased with the new Walter E. Heller Center when she attended the formal dedication ceremony with President Weil and Board Chairman Jerome Stone. Mrs. DeCosta is the widow of financier Walter E. Heller, for whom the university's college of business administration is named.

1972 The beautiful Michigan Avenue lobby was restored through a $100,000 gift from Edgar Kaufman, a professor of architecture at Columbia University.

not filled entirely by Roosevelt students, but as enrollments grew in the 1990's, the university took over the dormitory entirely. Most of the residents in the Herman Crown Center were international or students in the performing arts. With the economic and educational renaissance of the South Loop and the increase of enrollments of both international and out-of-state students, housing near the university has now become more desirable and attractive than ever – and, as we shall see, a major component in recent recruitment efforts to regionalize enrollments and attract students directly from the secondary schools.

Jerome Stone's greatest contribution was his leadership of three capital campaigns – "Up to Excellence," "Fulfilling the Promise," and "Threshold to Greatness." Shortly after the death of Walter E. Heller, who had been highly successful in international investment, Stone worked with his fellow trustee, Norman Mesirow of Mesirow Finance, in persuading Heller's widow, Alyce DeCosta, to name the Business College after her husband. DeCosta donated $2 million in 1970, which was the largest contribution the university had received until that time and supported the construction of a ten-story classroom, laboratory, and library facility in what had been a light and air court in the center of the Auditorium Building. In addition, her gift helped to modernize the eight story tower that Sullivan and Adler had originally designed for water tanks and that had provided hydraulic power for the elevators and lifts in the Auditorium Theatre. From this time until December 2000, when the business faculty relocated to the Center for Professional Advancement (18 South Michigan Avenue) and the Schaumburg Campus, the tower was its academic home and its programs were given the name of The Walter E. Heller College of Business Administration. Alyce DeCosta, who continued as a member of the board of trustees, also established the Walter E. Heller Lecture Series in International Business and Finance, which has featured Margaret Thatcher, Helmut Schmidt, Raymond Baer, Michael Wilson, Conrad

Open Discussion

Mutual respect between trustees and students enable both groups to meet to discuss the problems of the university.

Central photo:

Roosevelt University students and trustees are absorbed in discussion following one of several informal lunches held at the university at the suggestion of Board Chairman Jerome Stone, then chairman of the Executive Committee of Stone Container Corporation. The luncheons enabled students and trustees to meet and discuss university issues in a way that was beneficial to all.

Inset picture:

Trustee David Ferguson and President Weil chat with students prior to a 1983 luncheon. Ferguson later served as board chairman.

Portraits:

Pictured are some of the members of the Board of Trustees during President Weil's tenure whom the university depended on for guidance and leadership.

Dedicated to the Enlightenment of the Human Spirit

Norman Mesirow

Philip Klutznick

Max R. Schrayer

David Ferguson

Gerald Gidwitz

Robert J. Kamin

> America has the potential strength to wipe out every slum, to provide a decent education for every child, to combat ill-health and to provide equal opportunities for men and women of all races, creeds and colors. Our potential for greatness will not be reached until we have met those challenges.
>
> MARSHALL FIELD III
> IN A TALK AT ROOSEVELT UNIVERSITY

Black, Rolf Huppi, and other international figures who have delivered annual addresses before the Chicago business community.

These capital campaigns and DeCosta's generosity introduced Roosevelt University to traditional fundraising. Jerry Stone remembers one striking example that typifies the period:

Rolf Weil was president and I was chairman of a fund raising drive. We wanted to build on that awakening business confidence because as yet we had never attracted big dollars from the business community. So it was decided to contact Standard Oil Company, as Amoco was known then. Rolf and I made our first date with John Lind, who was the director of their foundation, and he was sympathetic to our plea.

He said, "However, I don't think our board understands completely what you're doing. I suggest that you set up a luncheon with some of our people and tell your story. Whereby, I set up this luncheon at the Standard Club (no relationship to the oil company) and Rolf made a brilliant presentation and spoke of the university not only in ideal terms, but pointed out the solid economies of a school that was giving excellent education for economic value. They spoke amongst themselves and during a break in the meeting, Rolf and I caucused. We had thought, originally, that if we got a pledge from a large industrial company that it would break the ice, so to speak, and were thinking in terms of $25,000 – $50,000. I told Rolf that I felt he had made a brilliant presentation that was well received and let's ask for $100,000. He was somewhat taken aback, but he agreed. "Well," they said, "we'll take it under advisement."

I wasn't sure whether we blew it, but we invited John Lind to our opening fund raising luncheon. And when he came, he brought a check for $25,000 and a pledge of $100,000. I practically kissed him, but I was able to take the story of the meeting and ended up by saying, "You expect more from Standard, and you get it!"

I won't say that was the beginning of a partnership that Roosevelt had with corporate interests. But in Winston Churchill's words, it was the "end of the beginning" when we could mostly rely on individual and foundation support. It was also the "beginning of the end" of sweating out finances because for the last 19 years [from 1971

– 1990 and in the years since Stone's address] Roosevelt had truly been a leader in college and university financial integrity having a balanced budget or surplus in all these years.

Jerome Stone left a distinctive mark on Roosevelt. In 1970, the university turned its Division of Continuing Education into a college named after his first wife, Evelyn, who died prematurely of Alzheimer's disease. The Evelyn T. Stone University College has become the home of the bachelor of general studies, external studies, hospitality management, training and development, on-line instruction, and a variety of certificate programs like Legal Assistance and non-credit courses.

The Bachelor of General Studies [BGS], which was first proposed at Roosevelt in the 1960's and established in the early 1970's was the central program of the Evelyn T. Stone University College. It was designed to appeal to working adults who wanted to complete their undergraduate degrees after having passed the traditional student age of 18-22. Adult education, as it was familiarly called, rested on the concept that people who brought significant life experiences to the university did not need to take as many required general education courses and could therefore pursue a shortened degree – approximately 80-90 credits instead of 120. The degree program had certain innovative features. It required every student to take a "pro-seminar" as a re-introduction to college study, a class that stressed writing skills and the critical interpretation of texts. The curriculum had interdisciplinary courses or what were called "integrating seminars" – a series entitled "Man and his Physical, Social, and Cultural Environments." Counseling was particularly important since many students were fearful of a formal education they had not completed years ago. And students were graded on a pass-fail basis. This continuing education degree was promoted by Lucy Marx and then

1969 Jerome Stone and his late wife, Evelyn, shared a moment following his election as Roosevelt's board chairman. In 1985, the College of Continuing Education was named in her honor and is now the Evelyn T. Stone University College.

1970 Amid much controversy, a new college, the College of Continuing Education, was created in 1970 to house the Bachelor of General Studies program that was designed for students 25 years of age and older who typically had been away from the classroom for several years.

George Dillavou, both of whom were influenced by Cyril Houle, a University of Chicago professor who was a seminal thinker in the field and received an honorary degree from Roosevelt.

The Bachelor of General Studies became highly popular – especially at Roosevelt where many of the students were over 25, the minimum age for students to enter the program. Surrounded by corporations in Chicago and the northwest suburbs which employed so many adults who had not completed their undergraduate education, Roosevelt was a university perfectly suited to accommodate the Bachelor of General Studies. But like so many non-traditional and unconventional forms of learning, it was highly controversial and was resisted by some faculty in the university community who had formal doctoral training in English, history, biology, and other core disciplines. Instructors in Arts and Sciences taught in the program, but a separate faculty soon developed who had the same traditional degrees but were non-traditional in their pedagogy.

The Bachelor of General Studies has clearly satisfied a growing constituency and has become one of the most important programs in the university, appealing to students whose achievements have matched or even exceeded those of traditional students. Educators have come to the realization that adults must be treated differently from undergraduates who have just emerged from high schools and colleges. By the 1990's, a significant part of the program was offered through the delivery system of Partners in Corporate Education, which takes the BGS program on site to corporations, at the convenience of employees. This adult degree program anticipated most of the modern forms of education – distance learning, on-line instruction, and continuing education – and bridged the divisions between the worlds of learning and work.

Always in search of additional enrollments, Roosevelt administered a computer science program in Hawaii and military bases in Germany and Spain that led to certification or a BGS degree. The program

1980's The Bachelor of General Studies Program has been tremendously successful over the years. It now is Roosevelt's largest single academic program.

1966 Vice President Hubert Humphrey visits with a student in Roosevelt's Upward Bound Program. A federally-funded activity, it provides training in English and math for underprepared or underprivileged students.

was operated under an agreement with Control Data Corporation. The on-site director and teaching faculty were Control Data employees, and classes were offered in a Control Data Facility. The College of Continuing Education had a Hawaii Program Advisor in Chicago who assisted students in making programmatic decisions. Teaching faculty and course syllabi were reviewed and approved by Computer Science faculty in Chicago, and the director as well as several administrators made periodic on-site visits to Hawaii.

The 1970's was a period when open admissions had a profound impact on higher education, and the democratization of learning prevailed in city and state universities. At Roosevelt the accommodation to underprivileged and underprepared students was made through several federally funded programs. The first was "Upward Bound," directed by Clifton Washington, a summer program that provided intensive, elaborate training in English, mathematics, and other basic subjects. Another was the Teachers Corps. In time, Trio, Veterans Upward Bound, Learning for Earning, and an elaborate Chicago Education Alliance which involved many other universities and the Chicago Public Schools would become important forms of public service.

These outreach programs were directed primarily to students from the Chicago public schools and naturally involved the education faculty, who were housed in a department in the College of Arts and Sciences. It became apparent by 1972 that the department had to be expanded into a college. Once again, there was resistance from the faculty of Arts and Sciences, but the vice president for academic affairs, Otto Wirth, was a strong advocate of a new College of Education and, more importantly, grants were becoming available from federal sources and local foundations that focused upon the improvement of primary education. Initially there was support from the Spencer Foundation, named after the former chairman of Roosevelt's Board of Trustees, Lyle Spencer, that led to the formation of a research

1977 Chicago Mayor Michael Bilandic (left) helps trustee Patrick O'Malley and President Weil unveil a bust of O'Malley in the hallway of the 180-seat O'Malley Workshop Theatre, which had opened on the seventh floor of the Auditorium Building in 1973. It has become tradition for theater students to pat the top of statute for good luck before they go on stage.

center in the College of Education. Soon practical programs in teacher preparation, elementary education, and secondary education were established. Later, in the 1990's, a doctorate in educational leadership would be implemented and the College would become one of the important leaders in reforming public education in Chicago. Indeed, one of every seven teachers or administrators in the Chicago Public Schools is a Roosevelt graduate, a dramatic example of the institution as a "private university in the public interest."

For higher education, the sixties and seventies were probably the most transformative decades in the twentieth century. Relatively inexpensive public community colleges and four-year universities grew in number and size and threatened private, comprehensive institutions like Roosevelt. In Chicago, the most striking development was the establishment of the University of Illinois at Chicago, one of Mayor Richard J. Daley's most significant achievements. Post-secondary education had been dominated by the University of Chicago and Northwestern, highly selective universities that drew students from across the country and the world, and by Loyola and DePaul, Catholic institutions that attracted a restricted following because of their religious orientation.

As the only private, nonsectarian, comprehensive university that appealed to local students, Roosevelt had enjoyed an audience of its own and was able to attract a diverse, multi-ethnic student population. But inexpensive community colleges in the city and suburbs were becoming more prominent; former teacher colleges like Chicago State and Northeastern were growing into four-year, comprehensive universities and charging very low tuition; Loyola and especially DePaul were broadening into institutions that attracted students of all religious faiths, and the University of Illinois at Chicago was evolving into a major urban institution that was directly competitive and offered an education at one-third the price of Roosevelt's. The distinctive characteristics of

1976 Roosevelt University celebrated the designation of the world-famous Auditorium Building as a National Historic Landmark by hosting a luncheon. Among those attending were trustee Alyce DeCosta and Edgar J. Kaufman of the Kaufman Charitable Fund, which supported the restoration of the lobby.

Roosevelt – social justice, diversity, affirmative action – were now common to these other institutions and the university was distinctly in danger of appearing historically important but out of step with current developments.

The change in the balance between full and part-time students during the period from 1965 to 1975 was the most significant result of the increased competition. Roosevelt went from having been a university with full-time students during the day to one that now enrolled increasing numbers of part-timers who came in the evening, after work. The highest enrollment the university ever enjoyed was 7,700 in 1976, but many of those students took individual courses rather than the four or five that would constitute a full-time program – the number 7,700, in academic parlance, refers to the "head count" of individual students as opposed to "full-time equivalent," which accounts for an average course load of 12 undergraduate and nine graduate credits as well as students in each class. Many of Roosevelt's students arrived from community colleges so that within a few years the university developed largely into an upper divisional institution that offered electives and specialized courses. In contrast to most colleges and universities, which require undergraduates to take 60 credits during their freshmen and sophomore years in a general education program and therefore can maintain average class sizes of 30 or more students, Roosevelt juniors and seniors went directly into disciplinary majors. New pre-professional programs proliferated to accommodate student needs, and the curriculum became increasingly career oriented, fragmented, and terribly expensive since the average class size was somewhere between ten and fifteen students.

The most dramatic example of the emphasis on professional training at the upper divisional and graduate levels was in the Business College. In the early years, the College of Commerce, as it was called, was distinguished by an accounting program led by Samuel Specthrie. From 1929 until 1946,

The Heller Lectures

The Walter E. Heller lectures bring to Roosevelt University individuals preeminent in the fields of international business and finance.

Dedicated to the Enlightenment of the Human Spirit

The Walter E. Heller Lecture in International Business was inaugurated in 1970 through a major gift from the Walter E. Heller Foundation whose president, Alyce DeCosta, is a Roosevelt University life trustee. The lecture series honors the memory of the late Walter E. Heller, Mrs. DeCosta's first husband, who was a leader in the field of international business, founder of Walter E. Heller and Company and a long-time friend of Roosevelt University.

Central picture:

In 1976, Great Britain's Minister of Education and Science Margaret Thatcher delivered the lecture. In 1977, she became the country's first female prime minister, a position she held until 1990.

Walter E. Heller

1974 Helmut Schmidt of Germany

2000 Rolf Huppi of Switzerland

1988 Raymond Barre (right) of France with Ted and Selma Gross and Mrs. Barre (left).

1996 Karan Singh of India

1986 Michael Wilson of Canada with Alyce DeCosta

1999 Conrad Black of England

1990 Etienne Davignon of Belgium

1976 Margaret Thatcher of Great Britain with Jerome Stone and Rolf Weil.

1972 Dr. Edwin O. Reischauer of the United States (right) greeted by Hugh H. O'Young, Consul General of the Republic of China (left) and Gerald Gidwitz.

1982 Jean-Jacques Servan-Schreiber of France with Jerome Stone (left) and Alyce DeCosta and Samuel Pisar.

Samuel Specthrie

> Man, being pre-occupied with 'things,' is becoming a 'thing' himself. We worship the things we produce.
>
> ERICH FROMM
> PSYCHOANALYST AND AUTHOR,
> IN A TALK AT ROOSEVELT UNIVERSITY
> 1958

Specthrie had been Professor of Accounting at Northwestern University, where he had received his MBA. He then came to Roosevelt and remained chairman of the Department of Accounting until 1970. Three of his books were widely used by students – *Mathematics for the Accountant*, *Industrial Accounting*, and *Basic Cost Accounting*. In addition to his scholarship and prominence in various organizations, Spechthrie was a beloved teacher. In 1962 he was named "Top Prof" by the graduating class and given a gleaming black silk top hat to commemorate the occasion. Stories about Specthrie were legendary, and his effect on students long-standing. By the time of his death in 1973, one tenth of all CPAs in Illinois had once been his students; of the 20 African American CPAs, 9 had studied with him.

When Specthrie stepped down as chairman of the department of accounting, the Business College had a clear image – it prepared students directly for careers. By the late seventies it constituted one-third of all enrollments in the university. Then an unfortunate set of events led to an internal crisis which affected the entire university throughout the 1980's. Although Specthrie set a high standard as a teacher/scholar who was incidentally a consultant to firms, he was surrounded for the most part by a faculty of working professionals who supplemented their meager Roosevelt income through extensive private practices in accounting, marketing, management, and other fields. Although these *de facto* part-timers were extremely effective in the classroom, they were not interested in becoming traditional scholars – and they were not always fully committed to the university. Several faculty members were authors like Specthrie, but most of them divided their time between their professional practice and the university.

In 1979, the College sought professional accreditation for its graduate school program from the American Assembly of Collegiate Schools of Business [AACSB]. The AACSB required extensive faculty research, library facilities, and released time for faculty to conduct scholarship; but the college was

1977 President Emeritus Edward "Jim" Sparling was 80 years old when this photograph (at top) was taken.

1981 A memorial service in Ganz Hall celebrated the vision and courage of President Sparling, the founder of Roosevelt University.

focused primarily on teaching and not prepared to meet these rigorous standards, which were geared toward research universities. The AACSB denied accreditation and then, to make matters worse, the university waged an unsuccessful lawsuit against the decision. The issue of the relative importance of scholarship and teaching was joined and would divide the faculty for years. The dean at the time, Douglas LaMont, and his successor, Ann Matasar, led the pursuit of accreditation in order to have the Walter E. Heller College of Business Administration join the ranks of other accredited business colleges, to gain status, to create a faculty that would combine teaching and scholarship, and perhaps most importantly to develop a community in which everyone was totally committed to the university rather than to outside careers. But the resolution of this debate was to a great extent predictable – Roosevelt could not afford the requirements demanded by that accrediting association.

The consequences of rejection from the AACSB and the denial of the university's appeal led to so severe a decline in enrollments that when the team representing the North Central Association – the organization that accredits the entire university – visited in 1986 they pointed to two major challenges confronting the university: declining enrollments and the lack of a strategic plan. That plan, when ultimately adopted, would lead to the resolution chosen by many other universities – Roosevelt would emphasize the primacy of teaching, reinforced by applied, activist research. Of course faculty would always be encouraged to produce works of traditional scholarship; indeed many works of distinction have been and will continue to be published. For fifteen years – from 1978 to 1993 – the Walter E. Heller College of Business Administration was divided between faculty who favored accreditation, which required resources for researchers, and those who emphasized teaching that prepared students for careers. The blurred focus of the college – and to an extent the entire university – became a serious issue.

The fiscal difficulties of the university were aggravated by the continuing deficits of the Auditorium Theatre, managed by a Council that increasingly sought independence but had not found clarity in its programming and had not solved the difficult problem of using this huge venue of 4,200 seats effectively. In 1981, the Auditorium Theatre Council created a corporate entity – the Auditorium Theatre Council Inc. – for fundraising purposes only. The Council wanted to separate itself from university governance, but Roosevelt would not sacrifice the theater and wanted the council simply to pay its own bills. The deficits of the theater accumulated to $400,000 by 1987 and were, of course, the ultimate responsibility of the university. Throughout the '70's and '80's the early admonitions of Leo Lerner seemed justified as the theater not only generated operational deficits but suffered, as did the Auditorium Building in general, from deferred maintenance.

From 1980 to 1988, the university conducted a $25 million fund drive which helped to mitigate some of these liabilities, but enrollments were still the critical factor on the balance sheet. Unfortunately, in the absence of a compelling plan, they declined from a high point of 7,700 students in 1976 to 5,800 in 1988, the number of full-time students declining proportionately even more. The University of Illinois at Chicago, DePaul, and Northeastern among other institutions were now competing aggressively within the city for those students who had traditionally come to Roosevelt. In 1988 the Chicago Public Schools that provided Roosevelt with most of its students were characterized by Secretary of Education William Bennett as the worst in the nation and the City Colleges, that once had graduated reasonably well-prepared students who transferred to Roosevelt, had declined severely in quality. The future of Roosevelt's Chicago Campus was troubled and unclear.

Weil and his administration were increasingly frustrated by this enrollment decline in Chicago and turned to the growing, fertile northwest suburbs for new enrollments. Lawrence Silverman, the Vice Pres-

1984 Anna Roosevelt of Chicago proudly displays a poster of her grandmother, Eleanor Roosevelt, announcing an event in the Auditorium Theatre to commemorate the 100th anniversary of Eleanor's birth.

> Unless workers are organized into bona fide trade unions of their own choosing, we cannot hope to establish social justice in the United States and we cannot hope to solve the problems of production and employment in the interests of the common good.
>
> PHILLIP MURRAY
> LABOR LEADER,
> IN A TALK AT ROOSEVELT UNIVERSITY

ident for Student Affairs, made a compelling case for a satellite in Arlington Heights. (Roosevelt previously had extensions at Fort Sheridan, Great Lakes Naval Base, Waukegan High School and Glenview Naval Air Station.) There were many fine public community colleges nearby – especially William Rainey Harper Community College, which would ultimately have 25,000 students – that satisfied the immediate needs of high school graduates and adults for an extremely inexpensive two-year, post-high school education close to their homes; but there was no college or university that offered upper-divisional and graduate study – there was no major college or university at all from Chicago to Rockford in the northwest or from Chicago to the Wisconsin border in the north. Enrollments at the first Arlington Heights site, the North Elementary School in Arlington Heights, where Roosevelt situated itself, grew so rapidly in the late '70's and early '80's that by 1986 the university rented 90,000 square feet in the former Forest View High School, the administrative headquarters of School District 214 at Goebbert Road in Arlington Heights. Albert A. Robin, a highly successful leader in construction throughout the metropolitan region, contributed $1 million in support of this initiative and the campus was named after him. Robin would supplement his initial contribution with other multi-million dollar gifts once the university found its permanent campus in Schaumburg.

Although the creation of a presence northwest of Chicago was prompted by the immediate need for more students, the campus would become profoundly important to Roosevelt's future. It would lead to the development of a metropolitan university with comprehensive centers in the city and suburbs that reflected the changing metropolis of Chicagoland itself. There was initial resistance by some suburbanites who feared that the university with its liberal tradition might bring larger numbers of underprivileged minorities into their middle-class white community, but it became clear that the primary purpose of the branch campus was to make

Fertile Suburbs

Recognizing a new market in the growing and fertile northwest suburbs, Roosevelt offered the only opportunity for students to study on a university level.

Roosevelt's presence in the northwest suburbs, prompted in part by the immediate need for more students, would profoundly affect its future. The expansion would lead to the development of a metropolitan university with comprehensive campuses in the city and suburbs that reflected the changing metropolis of Chicagoland itself.

Central picture:

From 1986 until 1996, the university rented 90,000 square feet in the former Forest View High School on Goebbert Road in Arlington Heights.

Pictured below from left:

In 1978 the Northwest Campus of Roosevelt University was established in the closed North Elementary School in Arlington Heights. Lawrence Silverman (left), vice president for Student and Metropolitan Affairs and Jerome Ellis, associate dean for Satellite Campus Programs, review plans for the new facility.

In 1986 the new Arlington Heights Campus was formally named for real estate developer Albert A. Robin. At the dedication ceremonies were, from left, Jerome Stone, Board Chairman Bart van Eck, Arlington Heights Mayor James Ryan, Robin and President Rolf Weil.

The Robin Campus attracted local residents eager for a university education close to home, and by the mid-eighties had 2,600 students in comparison to 3,200 at the Chicago Campus.

1986 Founder of one of the largest real estate firms in the country, Arthur Rubloff contributed half of his time to civic projects, including Roosevelt University where he was a trustee for 16 years. His will left $4 million to the university, which, in 1988, was used to create the Institute for Metropolitan Affairs.

education accessible to local residents, many of whom were frustrated by the absence of a university. The campus attracted local residents and by the mid-'80's had 2,600 students in comparison to 3,200 at the Chicago Campus.

The contrasts between the two campuses became dramatically clear. The city campus included 45% minority and 7% international students, the suburban virtually none. The city campus was dominated by less affluent students. The suburbanites were better prepared academically and more homogeneous in their ethnic and social background. The city students were in an architecturally renowned landmark, but it was 100 years old and needed repairs badly; the suburban students were at first in only a rented facility, but by 1996 they occupied a modernized 225,000 square foot building on 30 acres that the university purchased in Schaumburg, with state-of-the-art furnishings and equipment. At the outset, faculty did not want to drive to the northwest for their classes, but in time new faculty and even veterans enjoyed this second campus in the suburbs. It was modern; it was functional; it promised the future rather than cherished a past. Some staff at the Schaumburg Campus chafed at being considered the secondary citizens at a satellite campus; some at the Chicago Campus resented funds being appropriated for the build-out of the new facility in the suburbs. This unfolding story of two distinct campuses is described fully in the third chapter.

The real question was whether Roosevelt University would become like Chicagoland itself, a tale of two communities with racial and class divisions between city and suburbs. Although that scenario was ever threatening it would never develop completely, for the suburbs themselves would become increasingly multi-ethnic – initially with a greater presence of Hispanics and Asians – as Chicago became Chicagoland. As William Julius Wilson noted in *The Truly Disadvantaged*, middle-class blacks were beginning to migrate to suburban communities. At the same time, the city was improving the quality of

1990 President Theodore Gross and friends of the late Marvin Moss unveil a plaque naming a newly constructed gymnasium and exercise center after Moss, a 1949 graduate who became a successful Hollywood talent agent. Moss left $3 million to Roosevelt. His will specified that the university had to construct facilities to improve the social life of students.

The Moss Center exercise room, located on the fourth floor adjacent to the Herman Crown Center, is popular with students and staff. The gymnasium is above it.

its life dramatically and many suburbanites were migrating back to revitalized, safe and secure neighborhoods, with all of the cultural advantages and even an improved school system. The fourteen years of my administration, from 1988 to 2002, were blessed by a city whose quality of life was more attractive than ever before. The South Loop was totally transformed and the city itself became the university's urban campus.

At the end of his administration, Rolf Weil was rewarded for his patience in fundraising with two major gifts. Marvin Moss, a 1949 graduate, provided $3 million in his estate for fitness facilities which became an integral part of the Herman Crown Center. Moss felt that the students of the late forties had studied so hard in inadequate surroundings that they had not enjoyed themselves sufficiently. He had worked for the Music Corporation of America for many years and then became his own talent agent, amassing a considerable fortune. Although only a modest contributor while he was alive, he did remember Roosevelt in his will – and students have benefited enormously. Arthur Rubloff, the real estate leader, left $4 million that would be used for scholarships, an Arthur Rubloff Professorship in Policy Studies, and the establishment of an Institute for Metropolitan Affairs.

But it was evident that a strategic plan had to set new directions for the university. The absence of an endowment, the difficulties in balancing the budget, the deferred maintenance of the Auditorium Building and Theatre – these hard fiscal problems confronted the administration and caused it to avoid taking bold measures that would capture the suburban market while it was still free of competition, focus the course of study so that it did not attempt to appeal to every taste, or develop new programs that might suggest a coherent purpose. Meanwhile, other institutions – the University of Illinois at Chicago, DePaul and Loyola, Northeastern, and Chicago State – were growing into formidable competitors within the city.

1987 Chicago's business leaders decided to honor Mayor Harold Washington, who died unexpectedly in office, by establishing a Harold Washington Chair at Roosevelt University, his alma mater. Announcing the formation of the fundraising drive are President Weil; Robert Arganbright, head of the Amoco Foundation; Barry Sullivan, CEO of the First National Bank of Chicago; Eugene Sawyer, mayor of Chicago; and James Bere, CEO of Borg-Warner Corp.

1987 The entire Roosevelt community wanted to see actors Sean Connery, Kevin Costner and Robert DeNiro when they filmed the popular movie *The Untouchables* at Roosevelt. The Auditorium Building's famous lobby and staircase were shown prominently in the movie and the first-floor admissions office was used as a dressing room.

In 1965 Rolf Weil and his colleagues had inherited a university in perilous financial straits and given it stability, formed a real development office, established the five colleges of the current university, stood firmly and fairly during the student protests, built a residence hall, developed a board of trustees composed now of corporate leaders, and pointed toward further growth in the northwest suburbs. These achievements were significant, for they gave a traditional structure to the university and provided a foundation for its future. Now, as a third chapter was to unfold, Roosevelt would need to identify its distinctive profile in the transition to a new century. It would be a tall order.

The search for the successor to Rolf Weil was national in scope, involved the entire university community, and was staffed by a consulting firm. A committee of trustees, faculty, staff, and students was formed and chaired by David Ferguson, who had spent his career in public relations and who would become chairman of the board as well as the leader of a $45 million capital campaign, which successfully secured $53 million. The consulting firm analyzed the strengths and weaknesses of the university and recommended the development of a clearer, more focused sense of direction; the implementation of an effective strategic planning process; the strengthening of governance; the reversal of enrollment decline at the Chicago Campus; the updating of curriculum; the review of organizational and management practices; the revitalization of spirit and the sense of community; the strengthening of fundraising activities; the improvement of faculty salaries, and greater outreach into the black community.

A tall order indeed.

The search concluded in January 1988 with my appointment. At the time, I knew nothing of Roosevelt University and little of Chicago, except through the lens of Louis Sullivan, Carl Sandburg, Nelson Algren, and especially the Saul Bellow of *The Adventures of Augie March*. I had been awarded my

1988 After serving 23 years as President of Roosevelt University, Rolf Weil (left, at top) thoroughly enjoyed his retirement dinner. Board Chairman Alan Anixter offered congratulations.

Throughout President Weil's career, his wife, Leni, has been constantly at his side. The Weils first met in the early 1930's as youngsters in a Jewish youth group in Germany. They became reacquainted in Chicago, and married in 1945.

PhD at Columbia University in 1960, then written or edited fourteen books that focused on aspects of American Studies and education, and worked my way up the administrative ladder: chairman of a large English department, dean of humanities, and vice president for development at the City College of New York from 1958 to 1978, during the turbulent era of open admissions; provost of Penn State at Harrisburg from 1979 to 1983; and dean of letters and sciences at SUNY Purchase from 1983 to 1988. I had also spent several years at the University of Nancy as a Fulbright and then Visiting Professor and at other foreign institutions so that international education had a personal meaning for me.

I will never forget my Sunday afternoon interview in the huge conference room of the Westin Hotel at O'Hare Airport, when the former chairman of the board of trustees peered at me and asked: "Why do you want to come to Roosevelt University? It has no endowment. The faculty salaries are low. The Chicago Public School System and the City Colleges are in dreadful shape…." He went on with a recitation that was gloomy enough to discourage any candidate. My first response was a throwaway line: "I suppose I'm a glutton for punishment." Then I gave my real reasons: "I have been committed to urban education all of my career. For me, Roosevelt University is the private version of the City College of New York. As someone who was deeply involved in open admissions, I feel that mistakes were made when the college surrendered selectivity to open access. As president of Roosevelt I'll have the chance to help do it right – to recreate a university that balances excellence and access…Then there is Roosevelt's passion for social justice…Its belief in equal opportunity…The performing arts…The Auditorium Theatre…The location in the center of the city…."

I must have struck some chords in the search committee, for I was appointed in February 1988 and began my presidency in August.

A Metropolitan University

THEODORE L. GROSS

1988 Theodore Gross and his late wife, Selma, greeted guests, including former Board Chairman Jerome Stone, at a welcoming reception in the Sullivan Room.

1988 Board Chairman Alan Anixter (center) greets new president Theodore Gross (right) and retiring president Rolf Weil. Anixter said Theodore Gross's "proven administrative capabilities and outstanding academic accomplishments" were two of the reasons he was selected as Roosevelt's fourth president.

The 1986 accreditation report of the North Central Association had been a harsh review of the university. "Student enrollment is probably the most significant concern facing Roosevelt University presently and in the decade to come," it concluded. "Enrollment declines have affected all sectors of the campus, with surprising falls (approximately 25% in five years) in areas of business…The team recommends a Focused Evaluation be scheduled for 1989-90 to address two issues germane to Roosevelt University's continued capability to accomplish its purposes:

"1. Relationship of enrollment to the nature and quality of the institution's academic programs, and 2. Implementation of a long-range institutional planning, program evaluation and budgeting process, designed to both sustain and to allow the development of quality educational programs."

The report noted that "there was an 'atmosphere of trust' between faculty and administration that is encouraging to find during this period of managed decline at Roosevelt University. This positive atmosphere is due, in part, to the openness of key members of the administration, but also in large part to Roosevelt's long tradition of faculty governance. The underside of this satisfaction, however, is a certain amount of complacency."

I realized the gravity of these concerns and addressed them as aggressively as I could. I refused to accept the fate implied in the phrase, "the management of decline," a self-fulfilling prophecy that had created an institutional inferiority complex. I wanted to reverse course and articulate a goal of steady, controlled growth that resulted from clear planning.

I knew that effecting organizational change of the profound dimensions I had in mind depended upon a wholly new administration. Those in power seemed tired, defeated, and confused. My first decision was to establish the position of provost and vice president for academic affairs so that I would have a partner in designing a future for the university.

If I had to represent Roosevelt externally – developing the board of trustees, meeting people, and learning the philanthropic culture of Chicago – I needed a chief academic officer who could rebuild the university from within. I turned to Bob Graham, a former colleague of mine from Penn State, who began the difficult task of forging a strategic plan he called *Finding the Center*. The title was apt, for the task was like an archeological dig in which Bob and I – both outsiders to the culture of Roosevelt and Chicago – had to learn about the past and present before we could discover a future.

We needed a chief financial officer who would monitor the precarious financial condition of the university. Within a year, I appointed John Allerson, a senior vice president and controller at Norwest Bank in Minneapolis, who had never held an administrative position in a university. Allerson was a graduate in accounting from the University of Minnesota and had earned the highest score in Minnesota on the November 1975 CPA exam and the second highest in the nation among 42,000 examinees. He brought keen intelligence to this critical position, absolute integrity, and a conservative attitude toward fiscal matters that protected the university in each of its efforts to grow programmatically. Together with three provosts, he shaped a planning and budget process that introduced order and discipline to decision making and was a central figure in the purchase and development of the Schaumburg Campus and the Gage Building, named the Center for Professional Advancement. Allerson and I proved to be a productive team, as different as a New Yorker and Minnesotan might be – the visionary, idealistic, and aggressive president balanced by a sympathetic but pragmatic CFO. For thirteen years we worked together, commanding the respect of faculty, staff, and trustees, and most of the major projects that have shaped the contemporary Roosevelt University are at root a result of our collaboration and decision making.

1992 John Allerson, vice president for Business and Finance, improved the university's planning and budgeting process and oversaw a major expansion of academic facilities. Starting in 1994, Allerson was responsible for construction of the Schaumburg Campus, renovation of the Auditorium Building, expansion into the Gage Building and construction of University Center residence hall with DePaul University and Columbia College.

> Democracy is a harmony in which the beat of the drum and the melody of the flute are equally necessary.
>
> MADAM V. L. PANDIT
> INDIAN POLITICAL LEADER,
> IN A TALK AT ROOSEVELT UNIVERSITY
> 1959

Although Bob Graham consulted with deans and faculty committees in as democratic and exhaustive a fashion as possible, he was personally the chief architect of the first strategic plan, *Finding the Center* – a thorough review of the university that cost him his job. It was built upon four cornerstones: academic excellence; a progressive tradition; a metropolitan vision, and social responsibility. Graham developed the concept of "Centers of Opportunity and/or Excellence" that prioritized programs and then identified the resources needed to support them. Other programs have since been added to these – communications, teacher leadership, honors, risk management, real estate – but academic excellence for a metropolitan community, supplemented by outreach programs for the underprivileged and underprepared, has remained the educational balance we achieved at Roosevelt University.

Like me, Graham had been educated in the humanities and felt that the College of Arts and Sciences was marginalized at Roosevelt and needed to become the core academic unit of the university. Business claimed one-third of the student body, and Arts and Sciences had slipped into a loose federation of twenty-five small departments that served the professional programs. The College was fragmented and unfocused. Ronald Tallman was appointed as dean in 1991 and his most important accomplishment was the restructuring of the college into schools that were interdisciplinary: liberal studies, mathematics and sciences, computer science and telecommunications, policy studies, communication, and psychology. It would be a long time before these schools became truly interdisciplinary, but the structure was there; it would be some time before arts and sciences grew into the central college, but a new general education curriculum and later an honors program, Roosevelt Scholars, fueled the enrollments. When we decided to focus on recruiting students directly from local high schools, we established the centrality of the College of Arts and Sciences forever. For me, this shift of emphasis was critical to the creation of a

Finding the Center

Finding the Center was a strategic plan for the university built on four cornerstones: academic excellence, a progressive tradition, a metropolitan vision, and social responsibility.

Finding the Center was a plan to thoroughly review the university's academic programs and make recommendations about future directions.

Inset picture:

President Gross describes his vision for Roosevelt at a meeting of the President's Advisory Council at the University Club on April 18, 1989.

Pictured below, from left:

Robert Graham, provost and chief architect of *Finding the Center*.

President Gross and Robert Shepard, vice president for Development, exchange ideas before an Administrative Council meeting. Gross aggressively sought support from foundations and corporations.

Frank Cassell joined Roosevelt from the University of Wisconsin-Milwaukee. He helped make the Robin Campus an important cultural organization in the Northwest suburbs and organized the move into the Schaumburg Campus.

As dean of the College of Arts and Sciences, Ronald Tallman consolidated small academic programs into schools.

Robert Graham

Ted Gross

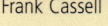
Bob Shepard

Frank Cassell   Ronald Tallman

1992 To connect Roosevelt University more closely with major issues confronting metropolitan Chicago, President Gross created the Institute for Metropolitan Affairs and appointed Richard Krieg, (right, at top) Chicago's commissioner of Public Health, as executive director. With him is Thomas Klutznick, chairman of the IMA's advisory board

1993 President Bill Clinton, flanked by Commerce Secretary Ron Brown and Labor Secretary Robert Reich, participated in a workplace conference organized by the Institute for Metropolitan Affairs. In addition to the topic of retraining workers for new jobs, the IMA also has produced action-oriented reports on education, the census, drugs, convention planning and the elderly.

balanced, complex metropolitan university. Now, under the leadership of Lynn Weiner, whose discipline is history and who served as Associate Dean under Tallman, the College has recruited young teacher/scholars and has coherence, balance, and prominence within the university.

The first major gift, which I inherited from Rolf Weil, was $4 million from Arthur Rubloff's estate. I used the funds to establish the Institute for Metropolitan Affairs [IMA] and thereby suggested the central theme and hallmark of my presidency – a metropolitan vision that reflected the growing interrelationships of Chicago and its suburbs. As I studied higher education in Greater Chicago, I could see that no other university possessed major campuses in the suburbs as well as the city. Those that had taken programs outside the city usually housed them in rented facilities and treated them as marginal outposts, as "cash cows."

Richard Krieg, who had been the Commissioner of Public Health, became the founding director of the IMA and worked with trustee Thomas Klutznick, who contributed a $1 million gift in support of the Institute and became chairman of its advisory board. The Institute connected the university with the civic concerns of Chicago and its initial efforts were impressive: a Mayor's Educational Roundtable; reports on drugs, violence and community policy, unfunded federal mandates, and convention planning; orientation seminars for new aldermen. Within a few short years, the IMA grew into an important research center for the university and the city and would, in time, reinvigorate the School of Policy Studies and the College of Arts and Sciences.

The College of Arts and Sciences

Finding the Center meant far more than rediscovering and reasserting the importance of arts and sciences. The self-study forced the university community to consider the vexing issue confronting all mainstream institutions like Roosevelt – the tension between academic standards and open access. Critical questions

2001 Lynn Y. Weiner, a historian whose book, *From Working Girl to Working Mother: The Female Labor Force in the United States, 1820-1980,* was nominated for a Pulitzer Prize in 1985, was appointed dean of the College of Arts and Sciences in 2001. She also founded the university's Center for New Deal Studies, a collection of books, articles and memorabilia focusing on Franklin and Eleanor Roosevelt.

1999 Roosevelt Scholars, an honors program developed by President Gross, has attracted high achieving full-time students to the university. Program director Sam Rosenberg (center) interviews each student before awarding him or her a substantial scholarship. At the heart of the program is a challenging curriculum with a special emphasis on metropolitan issues.

inevitably arose. Should everyone, regardless of academic competence, be admitted? Did centers of excellence imply elitism, racism, exclusion – and was their very creation a contradiction or betrayal of the original mission of the university? Should the university continue to be burdened by the necessity to teach basic writing, mathematics and other forms of pre-collegiate work? And what was the academic and financial cost of doing so?

For me, the resolution was clear. Roosevelt needed to become increasingly selective in its admissions as it grew steadily from 5,700 to 7,500 students over a 14-year period of time. Whatever support the university might give to underprepared, underprivileged high school graduates – and it would be extensive – would have to be in addition to credit-bearing programs. By doing so, faculty would have students in their classrooms who were more or less equally prepared, making teaching far more productive and pleasurable, and the university would not be saddled with expensive remediation that belonged in the high schools or community colleges. Most importantly, a clear academic policy would finally be fairest to the ill-prepared students themselves, for they would not be programmed for frustration or failure or lowered standards of an institution they would not respect. I had witnessed the revolving door of open admissions at the City University of New York from 1970 to 1978 that had resulted in so few students ever completing their baccalaureate degrees and the academic turmoil that had ensued for everyone. I vowed to myself that it would not happen at Roosevelt University.

The major effort to assert standards and selectivity and to increase the number of full-time students was the honors program, Roosevelt Scholars. In addition to the usual array of sophisticated courses, there were mentorships by trustees and alumni leaders and a core curriculum devoted to metropolitan issues. Within five years, the program had 120 full-time students and strengthened the College of Arts and Sciences considerably, casting a halo across the student body generally. The Roosevelt Scholars program was matched by other centers of excellence in a self-conscious effort to raise standards throughout the university. By 2001, the College of the Performing Arts increased its enrollments to 600 full-time, younger students and was, through its rigorous auditioning process, highly selective. In an innovative program with the Mid-America Committee (an organization of multi-national corporations), the Business College would recruit by the turn of the new century 120 executives from mainland China – extremely well-educated, motivated full-time students and their presence would create great prestige for the university throughout the city. The suburban campus would grow to 3,200 students by 2002, 700 of whom are full-time and well-prepared academically. These centers of excellence and opportunities have led to a tightening of standards as they have increased the student body and created a community of better prepared, full-time students.

The boldest initiative to strengthen the College of Arts and Sciences and the entire university was a program developed in 1997 specifically to attract full-time students directly from the high schools. Roosevelt had always been a university that primarily appealed to place-bound, non-traditional, community students, many of whom were married, all of whom were focused on career opportunities. Their average age was 29. The commitment to these older students continued, but by the late '90's a broad curriculum and full student services brought high school and community college graduates into classrooms during the day and created a much greater sense of community.

1998 The Albert A. Robin Campus in Schaumburg has four interior courtyards where students can meet and relax.

The Walter E. Heller College of Business Administration

The shift in the balance of power from business to arts and sciences, strengthened by a general education program that was required of all freshmen and sophomores, was essential to the health of the university. During this same period, the Walter E. Heller College of Business Administration began to find its

1996 Trustee C. Paul Johnson (right), CEO of First Colonial Bankshares Corp., presented a lecture on entrepreneurship for students in the Walter E. Heller College of Business Administration. With him, from left, are Dean James Cicarelli, President Gross, and Assistant Professor of Marketing Sumaria Mohan-Neill.

own focus. When I became president, the College had not yet recovered from its loss of accreditation in the early '80's. The faculty was still largely composed of full-timers who were divided between their outside employment and their commitment to the university, and part-timers with major professional obligations elsewhere.

The pursuit of re-accreditation by the American Assembly of Collegiate Schools of Business [AACSB] throughout the '80's seemed to me the quest for some kind of academic holy grail. The AACSB was extremely strict in its scholarly standards, requiring far more full-time, publishing faculty with terminal degrees who would demand reduced workloads, a library to support them, and other services the university could scarcely afford. Ann Matasar, who had been appointed dean in the mid-eighties, struggled to arrest the decline in enrollments that had been caused largely by the loss of accreditation. She made the case for AACSB accreditation even more vigorously than before, claiming that accreditation would create a halo effect for the other colleges and allow Roosevelt to compete with DePaul, Loyola, UIC, and other universities that already possessed professional certification. I shared her desire to raise standards and in the first two years of my presidency supported her efforts as much as I could afford to; but I soon saw that the university was unable to support fully credentialed faculty who were twice as expensive to hire as their counterparts in arts and sciences. Apart from the consequences to the morale of the faculty outside the Heller College of Business and my growing feeling that AACSB accreditation did not fit Roosevelt's mission, all of us soon realized that the university simply could not afford it.

Still, I wanted to try. With the assistance of a trustee, Fred Addy, the CFO of Amoco, we launched a $4 million fund drive for ten "named professorships" in accounting, marketing, management, banking, entrepreneurship, and other fields of business. The income of 5% from each $400,000 endowed professorship (or $20,000) would augment a budget line.

Trustee Leadership

The trustees of Roosevelt University provide leadership, financial support and wise guidance to the university's administration.

Dedicated to the Enlightenment of the Human Spirit

Roosevelt University has been fortunate to have some of the most distinguished civic leaders of metropolitan Chicago serve on its Board of Trustees. Leaders in their own careers, they share their wisdom selflessly and lend their stature to the university.

Central picture:

Alan Anixter, President Theodore Gross, President Emeritus Rolf Weil and Roosevelt trustees proceed to Gross' inauguration on April 19, 1989.

Inset picture:

James J. Mitchell III became chairman of the Board of Trustees in 1997. He was president of worldwide operations and technology for the Northern Trust Company.

Below at right, from left, some of the trustees who worked closely with Gross:

David Ferguson, public relations executive at U.S. Steel and Hill and Knowlton; Alan Anixter, co-founder of Anixter Brothers Inc.; Frederick Addy, chief financial officer of Amoco; Donald Hunt, president and chief operating for Harris Bancorp; Robert Mednick, managing partner for regulatory affairs at Arthur Andersen & Co.; Manfred Steinfeld, co-founder of Shelby Williams Industries; Sidney Port, founder of Lawson Products; and Albert A. Robin, founder of a Chicago construction company.

David Ferguson

Alan Anixter

Frederick Addy

James J. Mitchell III

Donald Hunt

Robert Mednick

Manfred Steinfeld

Sidney Port

Albert A. Robin

1990's Business Professor Joseph D. Ament started teaching at Roosevelt in 1966. A nationally known expert on taxation, he chaired the Department of Accounting and Taxation for 19 years and is currently the Samuel W. Specthrie Distinguished Professor of Accounting and Taxation. He also received the Arthur L. Crandall Award, given bi-annually to the most outstanding faculty member in the Walter E. Heller College of Business Administration.

At the very least, I reasoned, this campaign would be the preamble to a larger one I knew we would soon have to begin; at the most, it would attract credentialed faculty at higher salaries. Fred Addy was invaluable, for he raised the funds almost single-handedly from companies that had connections with Amoco. I will never forget the argument he used in my presence with his peers at the Amoco Foundation. It was compelling: "Why should Amoco recruit minorities from southern universities, many of whom return home after their first Chicago winter, when Roosevelt, with so many highly qualified African-Americans, is right down the street?"

The campaign was an immediate success and the ten named professorships helped to attract several qualified faculty; but they were not nearly sufficient to acquire accreditation. As we weighed the pros and cons of pursuing AACSB accreditation, we realized that it was financially out of reach and would drain resources needed by the other colleges. More fundamentally, the business college was emulating research universities instead of developing an organic sense of itself. That would come in 1996 with the appointment of James Cicarelli, who developed an MBA with 36 credits that allowed students to take traditional accounting, finance, marketing and management courses, and then concentrate either in one of these fields or in new programs like risk management, insurance, and financial services; real estate; hospitality and tourism studies, or non-profit management. Cicarelli also followed the pattern of the College of Arts and Sciences by dividing Business into several schools: Accounting, Financial Services, and Management. When Roosevelt located itself permanently at the Schaumburg Campus in 1996, the administrative offices of the Business College were placed there, in response to the reality that more than half of the students pursuing the MBA were from companies in the northwest suburbs.

By the end of the 1990's, the Walter E. Heller College of Business Administration was thriving and enrollments were growing at both campuses. In addi-

1999 Roosevelt's business college began a program in Risk Management and Insurance thanks to funding from several of the largest insurance companies in Illinois. Steven Tippins was selected to lead the program.

Marshall Bennett

Gerald Fogelson

Peter Linneman

2002 Three of the nation's most distinguished real estate executives, developers Marshall Bennett and Gerald Fogelson and educator Peter Linneman, helped President Gross create the Chicago School of Real Estate at Roosevelt, which became a separate school in the Walter E. Heller College of Business Administration.

tion to the innovative MBA program, three initiatives gave the College extraordinary new dimensions. A program in risk management, insurance, and financial services was launched under the leadership of Constantine Iordanou, CEO of Zurich US, a new trustee who also became chairman of the Community Advisory Board of the Robin Campus in Schaumburg and helped to raise $1 million from Zurich American, Aon, Kemper, American Express, and Mesirow. A Chicago School of Real Estate was established, with the guidance and personal contribution of trustee Gerald Fogelson, who worked with Marshall Bennett and me to build a multi-million dollar endowment. Fogelson was a brilliant entrepreneur who had developed, among many projects, Central Station for middle-class housing, just a few blocks south of Roosevelt's Chicago Campus. Marshall Bennett was a national leader in real estate and lent his great prestige to the creation of the Chicago School. He persuaded Peter Linneman, who had developed the real estate program at the Wharton School, to help to develop curriculum, appoint a permanent director and faculty, and raise an endowment for the Chicago School of Real Estate. A third program that strengthened the Heller College of Business Administration considerably was developed by Thomas Miner, chairman of the Mid America Committee, Toni Potenza, vice president for Administration, and the leadership of the Business College; they attracted cohorts of Chinese executives from Liaoning Province, Beijing, Shenzhen, Shanghai, and other provinces and cities for a one-year MBA in International Leadership. Within two years approximately 75 Chinese executives were coming annually to Roosevelt for the MBA.

The Walter E. Heller College of Business Administration has been reinvented and has now found its true center in the teaching and scholarship of business practices. Enrollments have steadily climbed; faculty with terminal degrees who are fully committed to the university have been appointed; and accreditation is now within reach from the

Association of Collegiate Business Schools and Programs, a more practically oriented accrediting organization, which fits the mission of the Business College far more precisely than the AACSB.

Evelyn T. Stone University College

1996 The Bachelor of General Studies, a time shortened degree program for adults, began in controversy during the late 1960's, but it soon flourished, and by 2000, it was the single largest degree program in the university.

1997 Roosevelt reached out to the Hispanic community in the 1990's by offering undergraduate courses in Logan Square and Little Village. A new home for the Logan Square Extension Center was dedicated by (from left, at top) student Erlina Jinete, site director Margarita O'Farral, University College Associate Dean Joan Lund, President Gross, Grace Methodist Church Pastor Margaret Gramley, and University College Dean Albert Bennett.

The unit of the university that has always been closest to the community is the Evelyn T. Stone University College. Its origins and development were resisted initially by the College of Arts and Sciences, for it offered a Bachelor of General Studies degree to students over the age of 25 that required 80-90 rather than the traditional 120 credits. The educational principle was that older students brought life experiences with them and did not need as many courses in general education.

It was not accidental that University College was conceived in the 1960's, a time of great experimentation in education. Its faculty was proud of being student centered, of teaching students rather than subjects, of emphasizing an interdisciplinary approach to learning, and of providing more counseling than usual. As higher education grew closer to the needs of working people and included those of all ages, it became clear that the adult student was in fact different from the high school graduate who wanted a campus life. There was virtue to the flexibility that tolerated "life experiences" in lieu of credits for those who needed to complete a degree in mid-career. Many of them were late bloomers and deeply appreciated a second chance to complete their degrees. The concept of life-long education was becoming more important and would be increasingly precious to those who worked while earning a degree and to those who retired and then, during their senior years, searched for cultural nourishment. There was the need for a college within the university that was flexible and receptive to experimentation, close to an external world that was changing more rapidly than ever before.

University College became a confederation of programs. At its core was the bachelor of general studies, the alternative degree for adults. It was also the home of hospitality management, made possible by a major gift from an alumnus, Manfred Steinfeld, who was the highly successful CEO of a company, Shelby Williams, that supplied furniture for hotels and restaurants throughout the world. The program grew into the Manfred Steinfeld School of Hospitality and Tourism Management and became one of the most popular in the university. The Evelyn T. Stone University College had a potpourri of other attractive programs: entry level work offered at an extension center in the Hispanic neighborhood of Logan Square; a masters in training and development; a Lawyer's Assistant program; an external degree that was the precursor of online instruction for those who could not be in traditional classrooms; and then the whole field of distance, asynchronous instruction. The College has become the institution's leader in online learning.

1991 Adrienne Hirsch, director of the Partners in Corporate Education program, explains how Roosevelt can advise and register students and teach courses at corporate offices.

The Stone College also became the home of Partners in Corporate Education, later renamed Partners in Education [PIE], a delivery system that brought course work to the corporate site, at the convenience of employees whose tuition was reimbursed by their companies. The curriculum for PIE began with a pro-seminar, a six-credit course that re-introduced the adult learner to higher education and persuaded him or her to continue taking courses at the campus itself. Originating with AT&T, PIE spread to 34 different companies in metropolitan Chicago. Under the leadership of Adrienne Hirsch, the program led to relationships between Roosevelt and local corporations far beyond credit-bearing courses. Zurich American, for example, contributed $1.6 million for a day care center that the children of its employees share with those of Roosevelt faculty and staff and the local community; it donated $250,000 toward a risk management, insurance, and financial services program, and gave $50,000 toward a Zurich American Alumni Hall at the Schaumburg Campus. Other companies that have participated in PIE – Sears, Motorola, Helene Curtis, 3 Com – have also been generous and become genuine partners with the university.

An Architectural Masterpiece

The importance of the Auditorium Building in the history of modern architecture is due to both the technical ingenuity of Adler and the decorative talents of Sullivan that made the building "sing."

The Auditorium Building, owned by Roosevelt University since 1946, is the major architectural landmark of the 19th Century in Chicago. Erected near the end of the Victorian era, it summarized the spirit of the age, introduced new concepts refined in the following decades, and remains as useful as it was the day it was completed.

The major figure behind the construction of the Auditorium Building was Ferdinand W. Peck. Through Peck, Dankmar Adler and Louis Sullivan were selected as architects. Peck secured funding for the building that was six times the cost per cubic foot of any previous building designed by the architects. As a result, the quality of materials and workmanship are outstanding. The good fortune for Chicago lay in the selection of the architects — Adler because of his engineering judgment, particularly in the area of acoustics, and Sullivan, who is now recognized as the creative architectural genius of the century.

Pictured at right:

Arch, detail in main lobby, an main staircase.

Facing page:

The former hotel lobby is now the university's lobby.

Partners in Education has now expanded into programs in school districts and governmental agencies. Laura Evans, the dean appointed in 1998, has given the college its focus in adult education and noncredit programs that have increased the enrollments dramatically. Coming from SUNY Purchase, where we had been colleagues, she has suffused a spirit of entrepreneurship not only in her own college but throughout the university and made all of us more responsive to the changing society.

The Chicago College of the Performing Arts

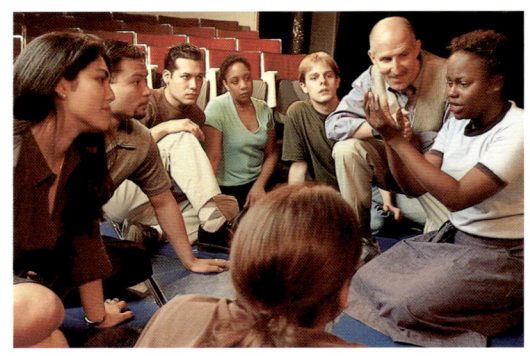

2001 Joel Fink, director of the Theatre Conservatory, teaches a class in the O'Malley Theatre.

The smallest and most selective of the professional colleges is Performing Arts. Historically, the theater program and the Chicago Musical College [CMC] had been separate. Theater was located in the College of Arts and Sciences, and Yolanda Miller, its leader for many years, did an exceptional job with limited resources of training students who performed in the O'Malley Theatre – a small theater-in-the-round named after trustee Patrick O'Malley. Miller laid the foundation for a theater program that was then developed by Joel Fink, who had vast experience in theater in New York and Colorado and expanded the enrollments to 220 students. Year by year, the entrance requirements grew increasingly selective, the students more talented, the visiting artists more illustrious, the program more prestigious. The O'Malley Theatre was refurbished into a jewel of a theater, a little stage surrounded by 275 seats in which performing miracles occurred.

The Chicago Musical College had been established in 1867 by Florenz Ziegfeld and was led for many years by Rudolph Ganz, a gifted Swiss pianist and conductor who came to America in 1901. During the early part of the century CMC was considered one of the great conservatories in the country, but it never secured an endowment or a great benefactor and by 1954 was in such financial straits that Ganz asked to have it acquired by Roosevelt as one of the five standing colleges.

From 1954 to 1987 CMC floundered and almost faded into memory because of the inherent expense of conservatory training. Then Earl Schub became dean and sketched out a ten-year plan that was clear and realistic. Schub had traveled from Brooklyn to Chicago and then to cities in California, earned an MBA from UCLA along the way, worked as public relations director at the San Francisco Opera, and returned to the Lyric Opera of Chicago before his tenure at Roosevelt. With a kind of steady resolution, creativity, and common sense, he led his colleagues into doubling the enrollments in a decade as well as improving their quality and then combined theater with music to form the College of Performing Arts.

The Chicago Musical College had been a financial albatross from the moment it was acquired, and the deans of the other colleges resented the disproportionate funding that the administration was compelled to give it. When I became president, I felt that music and theater could be the jewel in the crown of the university, its first great center of excellence. After studying the history of CMC and the magnificent Auditorium Theatre that was in the core of the building, I conceived of a conservatory which Chicago had not possessed since Ziegfeld's CMC in the early twentieth century, despite the existence of an orchestra and opera company comparable to any in the world. And when I was interviewed for the presidency, I was taken to the top of the highest balcony, up on the sixth floor of that 4,200-seat theater, and told to listen. A handyman dropped a quarter on the stage and I could hear the sound echo and echo in my ear. Perfect acoustics. I fell in love with it and saw the conservatory as part of a College and Center for the Performing Arts that included the Auditorium Theatre. I imagined performing arts as a hallmark of the university and a magnet for recruitment and fundraising.

Schub and I realized that tuition revenues would never balance the budget of the College and certainly not build the conservatory we had in mind.

2002 Students from throughout the world come to study with the outstanding instructors in the Music Conservatory in the Chicago College of Performing Arts.

2001 Ganz Hall, originally a banquet hall in the Auditorium Hotel, is used daily for concerts, lectures, and rehearsals. Roosevelt University has raised more than $1 million to restore the room, located on the seventh floor of the Auditorium Building, to its original grandeur.

1999 Betty Haag earned an international reputation for teaching youngsters to play the violin and other instruments by using the Suzuki method. Roosevelt acquired the Betty Haag Academy in 1999 and made it the centerpiece of the Community Academy in the Chicago College of Performing Arts. The award-winning Betty Haag Academy is located in the Metropolis Center in downtown Arlington Heights.

We turned to Marion Simon, who became my wife and chairman of a Chicago Board that was composed of 40 volunteers, to organize benefits that would ultimately bring in revenues of up to $1 million annually, attract 1,000 people to each event, and lend great prestige to the university. The roster of performers has included Itzhak Perlman, Marilyn Horne, Kiri Te Kanawa, Tony Bennett, Harry Belafonte, Bill Cosby, Frank Sinatra Jr., Michael Feinstein, Rosemary Clooney, Dionne Warwick, and Ramsey Lewis. Marion Simon is one of the great fundraisers in Chicago and has developed an annual gala that not only raises more money than any other of its kind but has brought the arts community closer to the university. The Chicago Board along with trustee Seymour Persky and other donors have refurbished and helped to beautify Ganz Hall, the lobby, the Sullivan Room, and other spaces in the Auditorium Building – and, at the same time, raised scholarships for student artists.

In 1999, the Betty Haag Academy was acquired by the university as a preparatory school within the Chicago College of the Performing Arts. Five hundred students from the ages of three to eighteen are in the Academy and have come each week with their parents to study the violin, piano, cello, and other instruments in a Suzuki method of instruction. Betty Haag is the finest practitioner of Suzuki in the country and has developed her Academy for the past thirty years. Under the auspices of Motorola, she and her students have performed at the Vatican and the White House as well as in Austria, China, Korea, Australia and other countries of the world. Now Betty Haag is approaching retirement and has brought her distinguished Academy to Roosevelt. It is situated in the new Metropolis Center for the Performing Arts in Arlington Heights and has plans to expand into other suburbs as well as Chicago itself.

Earl Schub was replaced by Donald Steven, who came from SUNY Purchase and appointed 25 principal players from the Chicago Symphony and Lyric Opera as master teachers. Steven was succeeded by James Gandre of the Manhattan School of Music, who is now embarked upon creating a premier board of advisors and building an endowment for the College. He and his colleagues have renamed the Chicago Musical College and theater program the Chicago College of the Performing Arts, with conservatories in music and theater and a community music academy that includes the Betty Haag Academy for the Performing Arts. The enrollments have risen to 600 and should reach 700 within the next several years at the same time as they become increasingly selective. Although the protracted litigation surrounding the Auditorium Theatre, described on pages 128-130, has cast a shadow on the ambitious plans for a center of the performing arts in metropolitan Chicago, the Chicago College of the Performing Arts now is becoming the leading conservatory in the city. Chicago has a great symphony, lyric opera, and summer festival; it does not yet have a nationally prominent school of music and theater. The Chicago College of Performing Arts will become that institution. It has indeed grown into the jewel in the crown of Roosevelt, a highly visible center of excellence, and a magnet for donors and students. Young artists come from across the world, and the conservatory now competes for them with Juilliard, Curtis, and the New England Conservatory of Music. Performing arts dominate the ninth story of the Auditorium Building. Students and faculty present their talents in Ganz Hall and O'Malley Theatre regularly and, as members of the Roosevelt University Orchestra, on the great stage of the Auditorium Theatre several times a year.

Seymour Persky

1999 The Chicago Woman's Club donated turn-of-the-century artwork, furniture and rugs to help restore the second floor Sullivan Room. A popular room for meetings and receptions, the Sullivan Room was the ladies' parlor when the Auditorium Building was a hotel.

Seymour Persky has been one of the most generous contributors to the ongoing renovation and restoration of the Auditorium Building, including the lobby, Sullivan Room, Ganz Hall and exterior. A well-known architectural preservationist, Perksy also is a 1952 Roosevelt graduate, real estate developer and university trustee. "I'm involved because I believe the Auditorium Building is the most important building in Chicago," he said.

A Vibrant Venue

Roosevelt University places special value on its music and theatre programs, gaining strength and inspiration from Chicago's many cultural attractions.

Roosevelt's Chicago College of Performing Arts provides professional training in music and theatre within the context of a vibrant university in a world-class city. Throughout its history, Roosevelt has emphasized the performing arts, and the quality of student productions has long been a source of pride to students, alumni and supporters of the university.

Central picture:

Each season, student productions in the O'Malley Theatre offer a stimulating mix of classics, contemporary plays, musicals, and experimental works.

Inset picture:

Music students perform in the beautiful and historic Ganz Hall.

Pictured below, from left:

Four of the leaders of Roosevelt University's music and theatre programs.

An annual gala to benefit The Chicago College of Performing Arts is hosted by the Chicago Board. The roster of performers has included Bill Cosby in 1999 and (at far right) Michael Feinstein and Rosemary Clooney in 2000. Since its inception, the event has raised more than $5 million for the College.

James Gandre
Dean of the
Chicago College of
Performing Arts
2000-present

Yolanda Miller
Director of the
Theatre Program
1959-1996

Earl Schub
Dean of the
Chicago Musical College
1982-1999

Joel Fink

Associate Dean,
Chicago College of
Performing Arts

Director of the Theatre
Conservatory

1997-present

International Students

1992 For several years in the early 1990's, Japanese students learned English in Japan and then came to the United States to earn their degrees at Roosevelt. The program, called Roosevelt University Japan, was established by President Gross and Japanese businessmen.

2000 During a visit to China, President Gross described the Executive MBA program to a top official in Shenyang. Groups of midlevel Chinese executives attend Roosevelt for one year to earn an MBA and learn about America. In addition to their studies, the students intern at corporations, attend sporting and cultural events and visit the homes of Roosevelt employees.

From the time of Roosevelt's origins, international students have always been a significant though small percentage of student enrollments – approximately 4-5%. My colleagues and I began to organize recruitment efforts that would increase the percentage of foreign students, for we recognized the globalization of higher education. With the aid of Japanese business leaders, Roosevelt University Japan [RUJ] was established in 1991 in a suburb of Tokyo; it trained Japanese students in English and then sent them to Roosevelt for a full course of study. Although subject to the vagaries of the Japanese economy, RUJ has been responsible for several hundred full-time students at the university. In Cyprus, the university appointed a Cypriot alumnus, Gregory Makrides, to be director, and he has succeeded in recruiting 15-20 students annually. The most ambitious recruitment effort has evolved from the partnership with the Mid-America Committee to recruit Chinese executives for a year-long MBA in International Leadership. These students have been sponsored by the government of Liaoning province and municipal agencies of Beijing, Shenzhen, Hongchou, Shenyang, Shanghai, and other cities. More than 300 have come since 1999.

Now 6% of the Roosevelt student body is composed of international students, and they form a vital part of the multi-ethnic, multi-national image of the university.

The College of Education

The College of Education emerged from Arts and Sciences in the early 1970's and developed an array of programs in pre-school, early childhood, secondary and special education, counseling and administration. Over the years, master's programs in teacher leadership and elementary education have flourished, and in 1995 a doctorate in educational leadership was initiated. For the past forty years, the College has been deeply involved in the welfare of the Chicago Public Schools – indeed, one of every seven employees in the system is a graduate of Roosevelt.

Although the education faculty publishes regularly in professional journals, and the doctoral program was a natural outgrowth of its interest in scholarship and educational policy, there has always been greater emphasis on field experience and pragmatic participation in the schools. Out of this deep involvement in public education has grown one of the most important projects in the College and the University – the Chicago Education Alliance. The Ford Foundation had developed a national project of urban partnerships between universities and public schools, geared toward retaining students in school and guiding them into college; in 1995, it provided a $3 million grant over a ten year period to establish the Alliance in Chicago. Participating institutions have included the University of Chicago, Northwestern, the University of Illinois at Chicago, Northeastern, Chicago State, DePaul, Loyola, the City Colleges – and Roosevelt, as leader. Most importantly, the Alliance also has had the active involvement of the Chief Executive Officer (Paul Vallas, then Arne Duncan) and the Chief Educational Officer (Cozette Buckney, followed by Barbara Eason Watkins) in the Chicago Public Schools, the head of the Principal's Association (Beverly Tunney), and a business leader (Martin B. Koldyke) who created programs like the Golden Apple in support of the school system. When I was at SUNY Purchase, just before coming to Roosevelt, I had helped to build a SUNY Purchase Westchester School Partnership of superintendents and college administrators through business, governmental, college and school funding. I was a strong advocate of the Chicago Educational Alliance and became chairman of its steering committee; but it was Teryl ann Rosch, the executive director, who was the active and creative leader, implementing a range of programs from screening school principals to teacher training institutes. The most notable and ambitious project thus far has been *Gear-Up*, a direct outgrowth of the Ford funding, and financed for $31 million by

1999 Secretary of Education Richard Riley came to Roosevelt University to announce a $31-million Gear Up grant to the Chicago Education Alliance, a consortium of colleges and schools led by Roosevelt. The grant enabled the colleges to help school children prepare for life after high school. Among those at the head table are President Gross and Teryl ann Rosch, executive director of the alliance.

1999 Roosevelt provides guidance on curriculum and offers advanced courses at Jones Academic Magnet High School, its neighbor in the South Loop. Principal Cynthia Barron and College of Education Dean George Lowery visit a class in the highly selective high school.

1995 A large cake shaped like the Auditorium Building was shared with faculty and staff as part of festivities marking Roosevelt University's 50th birthday. Television personality Bill Kurtis and Marion Simon (center), chairman of Roosevelt's Chicago Board, prepared to cut the cake.

the U.S. Department of Education. It is directed toward retaining students in the schools and encouraging them to pursue a college education.

The College of Education and the Chicago Education Alliance thrived as a result of the continuing emphasis placed on them within the university. Of equal importance, Mayor Daley had assumed personal responsibility for the Chicago Public School System and used the bully pulpit of his office to encourage leaders from all sectors to support primary public education as the centerpiece of the city's future. The revitalization of the schools has been one of Daley's great achievements and Roosevelt has been a distinct beneficiary. The university has been a partner to other key constituencies of the schools, other universities, businesses, non-profit organizations, and government. It has also developed a university-school partnership at the Schaumburg Campus. Superintendents of some of the finest school districts in the country serve on the community advisory board of the suburban campus and have welcomed the opportunity to organize an alliance with the university and local businesses.

Finding the Center was the first strategic plan of my administration and it led to the retirement of Bob Graham in 1994. He had worked with the deans and faculty to focus the curriculum, to find centers of excellence and opportunity, and to map a future for the university – but as often and extensively as he had spoken with administration and faculty, many claimed they had not been consulted. Graham's report was clear, cogent, and compelling; but inevitably it produced an adverse reaction from those who had not been identified for support or had been recommended for elimination. When he presented the report to the Roosevelt community on a Friday afternoon – what was called "the Friday Massacre"– he was sharply criticized and from that moment on was really not able to lead. With rare administrative courage, Bob Graham recommended fundamental organizational change of the kind that alters institutions fundamentally. There would be centers of excellence – music, accounting, psychology, marketing and communications – and centers of opportunity like hotel and tourism studies. But he was resisted and then resented. In time, most of the changes Graham recommended were implemented.

Bob Graham was followed by Stuart Fagan, who came from Fairleigh Dickinson University in New Jersey, and after five years of steady, pragmatic, and consolidating leadership, became the president of Governors State University. During his tenure at Roosevelt, Fagan developed an orderly strategic planning process and led the self-study for the North Central Association evaluation in 1996. By contrast with the critique a decade earlier, this NCA report found the university in strong shape, growing rapidly, and free of its two earlier problems: the absence of strategic planning and enrollment decline. Planning now informed practice, and

1998 The South Loop became one of Chicago's most desirable neighborhoods in the 1990's due to the construction of apartment buildings and condominiums, the opening of new restaurants and shops, and an influx of college students attending Roosevelt University, DePaul University, Columbia College, Robert Morris College, National-Louis University, the School of the Art Institute, and Harrington Institute of Design.

the enrollments had turned around. Indeed, the university was growing so rapidly in the northwest suburbs by 1995 that a site in Schaumburg had already been identified for a permanent campus. The most encouraging development was that Chicago was no longer viewed as a liability. It may have still been crowded with competing institutions, but it was already clear that growth was more than just a possibility; it was happening.

Much of Roosevelt University's success in the city during the 1990's resulted from a booming economy and a revitalized city. Chicago was experiencing a renaissance in which the South Loop was bursting with energy. The elements were extraordinary: an expansive Museum Campus (the Field Museum,

Stuart Fagan, provost, 1994-1999

Mary Hendry, vice president for Enrollment and Student Services, 1996-present

Vinton Thompson, provost, 1999-present

Antonia Potenza, vice president for Administration, 1997-present

Shedd Acquarium, the Adler Planetarium just south of the university near a reconfigured Lake Shore Drive). The new Harold Washington Library, one block from Roosevelt. A reconstituted State Street, with the beautiful and functional DePaul Center at State Street and Jackson Avenue and Robert Morris College at State and Congress Parkway. The return of middle class families to residential developments like Central Station and in condominiums or lofts throughout Printers Row. An expanded McCormick Place Convention Center, the largest in the nation, south of the university on the lakefront. Banks of flowers along the median of Michigan Avenue. A revived Cultural Center at Randolph Street and Michigan Avenue. The Symphony Center and Art Institute. If Michigan Avenue from Wacker to Roosevelt Road is "the cultural mile" then these institutions are the "cultural crescent." Even the public school system was beginning to improve under the leadership of Mayor Daley.

In 1996 I made one of the most critical appointments of my presidency. Mary Hendry came to the university as its Vice President for Enrollment Management (and later Student Services). She had enjoyed a brilliant career at St. Xavier University and introduced a contagious enthusiasm, appointing in turn young professionals who saw the recruitment opportunities in the city and suburbs and seized them. Recruitment, retention, and student services soon took on a whole new dimension. Hendry was absolutely convinced that she and her staff could build the enrollments at both campuses and within three years her determination was vindicated: student enrollments increased by approximately 5% annually, equally distributed at both campuses; the Herman Crown Center was occupied entirely by Roosevelt students; and the university expanded to five floors of the Center for Professional Advancement at 18 South Michigan Avenue (the "Gage Building"), a 12 story structure that faces the new Millennium Park and Lake Michigan. The Center for Professional Advancement increased instructional space by 40%.

As a result of growing enrollments and the attractiveness of Chicago, my colleagues and I initiated regional recruitment. Although Roosevelt had been primarily a commuter university for part-time transfers, we now recruited younger and full-time students directly from the high schools and community colleges, drawn to a city that had become safer and more secure and that was alive with cultural activities.

With Stuart Fagan's departure in 1999, Vinton Thompson, a faculty member for three decades who had been chairman of the Biology Department, director of the School of Science and Math and Chair of the Faculty Senate, became acting provost. It was a natural transition since Thompson had served as Fagan's associate provost and was the key leader of master plans for the reconfigured facilities in the Auditorium Building and the Center for Professional Advancement at 18 South Michigan Avenue.

Two of the most important achievements of the 1990's were the dramatic development of a board of trustees that now represented the highest level of corporate leadership and the implementation of a $45 million capital campaign that concluded by having raised (with the guidance of the Development office) $53 million. After Jerome Stone had stepped down as chairman in 1983, he was succeeded briefly by Bart van Eck, a vice president at FMC, and then by Alan Anixter. Anixter had made his fortune through a cable and wiring distribution company that was ultimately sold to Itel. During the next few years, I made a concerted effort to recruit the most senior level executives from the Tribune Company, Sears, Motorola, Sara Lee, and various banks in the city. I knew that the CEOs themselves were almost automatically recruited by the University of Chicago and Northwestern so I approached younger, rising vice presidents who truly cared about an institution like Roosevelt and who were destined for leadership roles in their own companies. They became crucial to my major initiatives: the capital campaign and the purchase of the Schaumburg Campus.

1993 A U.S. postage stamp honoring the famed chemist Percy Lavon Julian, who synthesized cortisone for arthritis, was unveiled at Roosevelt University. Dr. Julian was a Roosevelt trustee from 1945 until his death in 1975. Members of Julian's family presented a photograph of the stamp to President Gross. The picture hangs in the second floor hallway.

1996 Myrtle Shannon, the oldest graduate in the history of the university at age 92, visits with some of her classmates. Three days after receiving her diploma, Shannon, a history major, attended a Roosevelt University job fair.

Campaigns and Gifts

Donations from private and public organizations are the lifeblood of private universities. They support the programs and facilities necessary to educate the next generation of leaders.

More than 5,000 friends, alumni, foundations, corporations and community organizations contributed to the Renaissance Campaign, which ran from 1992 until 1997. The campaign raised $53 million, $8 million more than the goal, making it the most successful fundraising drive in the history of Roosevelt University. The Renaissance Campaign supported the new Albert A. Robin Campus, endowed chairs in the business college, the hospitality management program, a chair in urban education, scholarships, the Auditorium Theatre, the Institute for Metropolitan Affairs and other needs.

Central picture:

Trustee David Ferguson, former vice president for public relations at U.S. Steel, chaired the Renaissance Campaign.

Below, from left:

In 2000 Florence Miner, a Roosevelt alumna, gave the university its single largest gift which was used for the School of Computer Science and Telecommunications. At a reception in her honor are Robert Galvin (left), former CEO of Motorola where Ms. Miner worked, and President Gross.

In 1998, Robert Cushing, president of Pepsi General Bottlers, presented President Gross with a $1 million check for student scholarships.

Ruth Benton, Roosevelt's first female vice president, organized the Renaissance Campaign, which was completed by her successor as vice president for development, Ronald Champagne.

Ruth Benton

Ronald Champagne

Frederick Addy | Alan Anixter | David Hiller

Constantine Iordanou | James J. Mitchell III | Sidney Port

Albert A. Robin | Melvin Katten | Kenneth Tucker

Alan Anixter was responsible for my appointment and rallied behind me in setting the stage for the largest fund drive in the university's history. David Ferguson, who had retired from a successful career as vice president of public relations for U.S. Steel and now was a consultant to Hill and Knowlton, led the campaign. He had headed up the presidential search committee in 1987 and became board chairman several years later. The major contributions of the campaign included million dollar gifts from Al Robin, for whom the suburban campus was named; Manfred Steinfeld, who had helped to create the School of Hospitality and Tourism Management; and Thomas Klutznick, who worked with Richard Krieg to organize the Institute for Metropolitan Affairs. By 1992, when the campaign was officially launched, the board was represented by corporate leaders who delivered six-figure company gifts that formed the foundation of the campaign. The leading example was Fred Addy, chief financial officer of Amoco, who had raised the $3 million for named professorships in the business college, which includes a $400,000 gift from Amoco, and succeeded Anixter as chairman of the board.

Although the campaign featured the usual elements of endowed chairs, scholarships, and programmatic support, at its heart was the purchase of 30 acres in Schaumburg, dominated by a 225,000 square foot building, that would form a permanent campus in the northwest suburbs. We had identified the site that was occupied by the midwest headquarters of the Unocal Corporation for several decades, and developed a plan for acquisition and conversion of the property. The entire project was estimated at $21.5 million, $5 million of which was to be raised as part of a $45 million capital campaign, and $16.5 million covered by a bond issue.

Since the university had not yet developed major donors in the northwest suburbs, it had to rely upon the trustees for support. Al Robin, who had already given $1 million for the temporary site in Arlington Heights, made an additional pledge; Sidney Port,

> The constitutional guarantees of individual freedom...were designed to elevate the liberty of the individual even though the incidental effect was to make the conviction of the guilty more difficult.
>
> HON. HUGO L. BLACK
> SUPREME COURT JUSTICE,
> IN A TALK AT ROOSEVELT UNIVERSITY

who has been one of the major donors throughout my administration, made a significant contribution and the Plaza in front of the building bears his name. Other trustees stepped to the plate. Kenneth Tucker has a board room named after him; Constantine Iordanou, CEO of Zurich US, provided $1.6 million from the corporation for a day-care center and additional funds for an alumni hall; David Hiller, senior vice president of the Tribune Company, helped to secure a $500,000 major gift from the McCormick Tribune Foundation to name the electronic library; and, perhaps most importantly for the future development of the campus, an emerging community advisory board raised funds from small and mid-size companies in the northwest suburbs. The development office had succeeded in securing a $750,000 grant from the Kresge Foundation, which was a 3-1 challenge to widen the base of alumni and community support. By 1997, when the development drive ended, more than $5 million was raised for the Robin Campus and the $45 million goal for the entire capital campaign was surpassed – the ultimate amount of money that came to the university was $53 million.

The first building phase included 150,000 square feet, and the classrooms were soon filled with almost 2,700 students, most of them simply transfers from the rented facilities in Arlington Heights. The establishment of the Albert A. Robin Campus in Schaumburg, as I repeated throughout the capital campaign, was the most important event in the history of the university since Roosevelt moved into the Auditorium Building in 1947. Beyond being a smart move to an area where no comprehensive university existed, at the geographic crossroads of the northwest suburbs, it represented the physical expression of our metropolitan vision.

Toward the end of the $53 million campaign, Ronald Champagne was appointed as vice president of Development. He had been president of St. Xavier University for twelve years and had considerable experience in raising funds from major donors and in lobbying the state and federal governmental agencies for capital construction projects. Together with his colleagues, Champagne secured large gifts for a chemistry laboratory and classrooms in the Auditorium Building; he modernized technology within the development office, and perhaps most importantly increased alumni support and planned giving. One dramatic example of his efforts was a multi-million gift in the summer of 2000 from Florence Miner, the sister of the co-founder of Oracle Corporation, that supported the development of a major School of Computer Science and Telecommunications. It was the largest contribution in the history of the university and marked a new level of fundraising. In 2001, the development office secured more than $15 million, setting a benchmark for annual giving.

2000 A press conference to announce Florence Miner's gift to Roosevelt was held in a new computer classroom at the Albert A. Robin Campus in Schaumburg. As President Gross and Ms. Miner looked on, Raymond Wright, director of the School of Computer Science and Telecommunications, explained how students in his school would benefit from her multi-million contribution, the largest in the history of the university.

One important dimension of fundraising was programmatic and a sequel to the curricular support provided by the Renaissance campaign. We called it Renaissance II. We had concluded that a $5 million trustee campaign of funding for ten highly popular programs – communication, education, psychology, the Bachelor of General Studies – would increase enrollments swiftly and lift them across the entire university. James J. Mitchell III, who had become chairman of the board when David Ferguson died in 1998, assumed the leadership role of Renaissance II. Not only did he make a lead gift, but he championed the effort and worked with Champagne and me to make it a success. Jim Mitchell has been an ideal chairman, a creative leader as Roosevelt enters the new century. The former president of Worldwide Operations and Technology at Northern Trust, he understands the importance of enrollment growth and has encouraged the build-out of the Schaumburg Campus, the development of the Center for Professional Advancement at 18 South Michigan Avenue, and our many programmatic initiatives.

Frank Cassell, who had come from the University of Wisconsin at Milwaukee in 1991 to lead the

1994 Frank Cassell (far right), chief executive of the Robin Campus, organized the university's move from Arlington Heights to Schaumburg. Through his vision and leadership, Roosevelt became the first university in the populous northwest suburbs to own a building and offer comprehensive university services. After he left to become president at the University of Pittsburgh/Greenburgh, the campus was managed by John Joseph from 1997 until 2000 and Michael Durnil since 2000.

John Joseph

J. Michael Durnil

Schaumburg Campus, was its dynamic leader and academic architect. He built a strong community advisory board; he worked with John Allerson to design the campus; and he established Roosevelt as the major university in the northwest suburbs. After the campus was opened in 1996, Cassell went on to become the president of the University of Pittsburgh at Greenburgh and was succeeded by John Joseph, who had served as executive assistant to the president, vice president for development and then vice president for administration. Joseph strengthened Roosevelt's ties to the community and initiated efforts to attract full-time students during the day and develop distance learning and on-line instruction. He became president of the University of Maine at Machias in 2000 and was succeeded by J. Michael Durnil, who had been a highly successful associate vice president for student services. Durnil now serves as executive officer of a campus that has turned its attention to the recruitment of more day students directly from local high schools. He has taken on the responsibility of designing its master plan. It will be a comprehensive campus that will ultimately accommodate at least 4,000 students and offer an entire curriculum – except for performing arts – that allows students in the northwest community to take all of their courses there, within a few miles of their home or their work site. The Schaumburg Campus has become a university for the burgeoning northwest community.

The decision to purchase the 27-acre campus in Schaumburg was made in January of 1995, as Unocal pressed Roosevelt to negotiate a contract. The trustees were convinced that this opportunity in the northwest suburbs had to be seized, but many of the faculty and some administrators were fearful. Resources were scarce, and everyone knew it. As compelling as the case for the Schaumburg Campus was, the administration realized that it could not neglect the deferred maintenance of the Auditorium Building or the appointment of faculty and staff to build upon the enrollments that were now beginning

Robin Opens!

The establishment of the Schaumburg Campus proved to be the wisest decision the university ever made, after the purchase of the Auditorium Building.

Dedicated to the Enlightenment of the Human Spirit

Roosevelt University celebrated the grand opening of its new Albert A. Robin Campus in Schaumburg on August 17, 1996. The only comprehensive university in the northwest suburbs, the facility became highly popular with students and members of the community. As of 2001, enrollment stood at more than 3,200 students.

Central picture:

Those participating in the formal ribbon-cutting ceremony were (from left), John Allerson, vice president for Business and Finance; Stuart Fagan, provost; Antonia Potenza, vice president for Administration; Rolf Weil, former president; David Ferguson, chairman of the Board of Trustees; Peter Smith, president of the Robin Campus Community Advisory Board; Rita Mullins, mayor of Palatine; Frank Cassell, executive officer of the Robin Campus; Arlene Mulder, mayor of Arlington Heights; Al Larson, mayor of Schaumburg; Terry Parke, state representative; Ted Gross, president; and Albert A. Robin, benefactor.

Below, from left:

The main entrance to the building is a popular gathering spot for students.

Albert A. Robin declares, "The campus is open!"

to grow. The American National Bank and Trust Co. of Chicago, which was to provide credit enhancement for new bonds, insisted that $5 million in cash be shown if it were to underwrite a $16.5 million bond issue. Pledges had been made by corporations and individual donors, but the required cash was not in hand – and Unocal insisted upon closing the deal by the end of 1994. In order to persuade the trustees and the bank that purchase of the Schaumburg Campus was viable, I turned to the Auditorium Theatre Council [ATC], which had accumulated $3.2 million in cash reserves as a result of the highly successful runs of *Les Miserables, Phantom of the Opera*, and *Miss Saigon*, and requested that $1.5 million be temporarily transferred to the university's account so that the campus in Schaumburg could be purchased. I promised that the funds would be replaced once pledges that had already been made came through.

From the point of view of the university, the request seemed justified. Roosevelt owned the Auditorium Theatre; the Council was an operating committee of the Board of Trustees; and I was simply asking that funds be transferred from one unit to another. But even before I made the formal request, I knew that there would be a confrontation. I had been elected as chairman of the ATC in the early 1990's when council members had acquiesced to Roosevelt's nominal control of the theater; but for thirty years they had sought – and sought even more forcibly now – to keep themselves as independent of the university as possible. After two decades, during which the Auditorium Theatre had operated at a deficit and borrowed funds from the university simply to remain open, the Council appointed Dulcie Gilmore in 1987 as executive director. Gilmore brought in major Broadway shows and used the revenues to refurbish the theater and develop a reserve fund. As the Theatre became successful, the ATC saw itself as increasingly autonomous and independent of the university.

As soon as I made the request for a transfer of monies, at a tempestuous meeting on December 15,

1992 Under the leadership of Executive Director Dulcie Gilmore, the Auditorium Theatre during the late 1980's and early 1990's was the Midwest venue for *Les Miserables, The Phantom of the Opera* and *Miss Saigon*. President Gross served as chairman of the Auditorium Theatre Council. In December 1994, the Auditorium Theatre Council sued Roosevelt University over control of the theatre, setting off a public court battle that has lasted for more than seven years.

1994, I was refused. Fred Eychaner, a wealthy entrepreneur who served on the executive committee of the ATC, and Bettylou Weiss, a relative by marriage of Bea Spachner, filed a lawsuit that afternoon to prevent the university from accessing the reserve funds of the theater. For the next eight years, the Council and the university engaged in litigation. Various attempts have been made at settlement, but in every instance, majority control of the Auditorium Theatre has become the issue. Roosevelt claimed that the university owned the Auditorium Theatre, it was a unit of the university from the time Roosevelt had bought the Auditorium Building, and the trustees finally governed it. ATC asserted that the theater was independent and held in trust for the people of Chicago. In September 1998, after a ten-week bench trial, Judge Aaron Jaffe of the Circuit Court issued a 75-page opinion that indicated the university not only owned the theater but had authority over its assets and operations. This order was appealed and remanded to the circuit court again for corrections of Jaffe's order. Roosevelt appealed that decision to the Supreme Court of Illinois and now awaits a final verdict.

The Auditorium Theatre litigation cost both sides large amounts of time and legal fees. But equally damaging was the persistent effort of the ATC to create the impression that Roosevelt was taking $1.5 million permanently from the account of a theater that was finally prospering and using it to purchase a campus in Schaumburg. The Council hired a public relations firm and waged a campaign against the university that focused on Roosevelt's ostensible abandonment of Chicago and its purported use of theater revenues for university purposes. I became the scapegoat and was demonized as the determined leader who simply wanted to take advantage of the theater now that it was profitable. It took a good deal of courage and discipline to ignore these personal criticisms and avoid public confrontations, but I believed deeply in the university's position. Restraint was particularly difficult since tuition

1994-2002 The battle for control of the Auditorium Theatre was waged in the Circuit Court, Appellate Court and the Illinois Supreme Court.

> Human beings are…born wholly equipped and extremely well organized to function from the very beginning as loving, cooperative creatures who require nothing more, in fact, than to receive the developmental stimulation that love provides.
>
> ASHLEY MONTAGUE
> ANTHROPOLOGIST,
> IN A TALK AT ROOSEVELT UNIVERSITY
> 1954

from struggling students had subsidized deficit budgets during the theater's darkest fiscal days of the '70's and '80's. Forty percent of the Auditorium Building – the core of this great structure – was occupied by the theater. Just as Louis Sullivan and Dankmar Adler knew that the hotel and theater were interdependent so too were the university and its performing arts space. The trustees had never intended to separate the Auditorium Theatre from Roosevelt University. The Auditorium Theatre Council had simply created its own sense of autonomy. I shared President Sparling's original vision of a great Center for the Performing Arts for the public, associated with a first-rate conservatory of music and theater. One of the reasons I was able to sustain my vision and belief was that the entire Roosevelt University community – and especially the Board of Trustees – stood unanimously behind me.

Once the lawsuit was filed on December 15, 1994, the university borrowed the additional $1.5 million with additional support from American National Bank & Trust Co. and proceeded to purchase and develop the Schaumburg Campus. As it turned out, no funds were ever taken from the Auditorium Theatre coffers.

The purchase of the Schaumburg Campus proved to be one of the wisest decisions the university ever made. In the northwest and western suburbs there are many large, excellent public community colleges – Harper, Oakton, Triton, Lake County, Elgin, DuPage. There are also individual universities – Northern Illinois in Hoffman Estates and DePaul in Des Plaines and Rolling Meadows – that offer specific programs in business or computer science, and there are small denominational colleges that dot the landscape. But there is no university that has established a major campus which provides all the services of a comprehensive university. This region on the outskirts of Chicago extends as far west as Rockford and as far north as Milwaukee and includes some of the finest school districts in the

1994 Roosevelt's campuses in both Arlington Heights and Schaumburg were named for real estate developer Albert A. Robin, whose generous contributions made them a reality. This plaque, which originally hung in Arlington Heights, is now on the exterior of the campus in Schaumburg near the front door. Frank Cassell, chief executive of the Robin Campus, and President Gross hosted a reception to thank Robin for his gifts.

1960's The Albert A. Robin Campus is strategically located in Schaumburg at the intersection of Golf and Meacham Roads. Roosevelt acquired the closed regional headquarters of Unocal Corporation (pictured above) in 1994 and converted the building into a modern university campus. The property surrounding the Unocal facility has been completely developed.

state. It also is an area that boasts major corporations: Motorola, Sears, Zurich US, Allstate, Baxter, Abbott, United Airlines and 3 Com in the north and northwest; Lucent, Molex, TellLabs, and Servicemaster in the west – and scores of mid-size and small businesses, a thriving place where the frontier between city and suburbs is metamorphosing into a metropolis that has not yet defined itself fully. Schaumburg is the second largest edge city in the nation and a major part of the northwest suburbs.

And at the center of this new frontier is Roosevelt University. As resources became available, the university completed the main building by developing more classrooms, a student union and cafeteria; then it designed a master plan for the 30-acre campus that included another classroom building which featured computer science and telecommunications; a parking deck, and a multi-purpose facility for student residences, a fitness center, and other structures. It will take years for all these buildings to be constructed, but there is a clearly articulated plan and the campus has already become the university for this community, satisfying the needs of sophisticated, ambitious, placebound students for undergraduate and graduate degrees, of adults who crave continuing education, of business leaders who need to keep their workforce *au courant* – and now a university campus for undergraduates coming directly from local and regional high schools.

The university had always been largely dependent upon transfer students from local community colleges, students supported by their companies' tuition reimbursement programs and by non-traditional students who returned to complete their degrees. These were older students who could not leave the region for an expensive education in a private college and who crowded the classrooms during the evenings. We knew there were also large numbers of traditional aged students who could be persuaded to come directly to the Chicago and Schaumburg campuses from their high schools rather than attend community colleges first. The admissions office

Lobby of the Auditorium Building.

Entrance to the Schaumburg Campus.

began to recruit heavily in the high schools, offering scholarship aid that reduced the tuition difference between the community colleges and Roosevelt – and the number of new students increased dramatically. That effort led to regional recruitment, which promoted performing arts, hotel and tourism studies, communications, arts management, and other programs and welcomed high school graduates as well as nontraditional and transfer students. There was an initial fear that Roosevelt would become a bimodal university, with distinct student populations during the day and evening; but the different types of students soon interacted and shared each other's classes, nurturing one another in unpredictable ways. More than ever before, Roosevelt University became an inter-generational university.

We recruited high school graduates for many reasons. It was obvious that classrooms and other facilities were filled to capacity in the evening but half empty in the mornings and afternoons – the physical plant was not being used sufficiently. Then, demographers were predicting that there would be a significant increase of high school graduates in the new century, and many of them could not afford the high price of tuition in private colleges and universities or would not leave home for personal reasons. Finally, Chicago, the northwest, and western suburbs were experiencing extraordinary growth and prosperity, and becoming more and more attractive to young people throughout the midwest.

The explosive expansion of the suburbs was a sociological and cultural phenomenon of profound proportions for metropolitan Chicago at the turn of the new century. Where there had been cornfields and prairies only a few years before, there were cities and villages and corporate towers and shopping malls and highways crisscrossing the landscape in ways that formed a new type of campus for a university that would continue to take education to corporate sites and to schools and that would use distance learning and all forms of technology. It would be a university for the community, relating to the schools

2001 Roosevelt's Board of Trustees gave its approval for the university to participate in University Center of Chicago, a 1,720-bed residence hall to be built jointly by Columbia College, DePaul University and Roosevelt. University Center will be located on a city-owned parking lot. Planned to open in the fall of 2004, the facility will allow Roosevelt to attract more full-time students from outside metropolitan Chicago.

2002 Chicago Mayor Richard M. Daley participated in groundbreaking ceremonies for University Center of Chicago, which will be located on the southeast corner of State Street and Congress Parkway. From left to right are Theodore Gross, president of Roosevelt University; John Allerson, vice president of business and finance at Roosevelt; Warrick Carter, president of Columbia College; Ken McHugh, executive vice president of operations at DePaul University; Alderman Burton Natarus; Mayor Daley; and Rev. John P. Minogue, president of DePaul.

and government agencies and businesses and becoming their educational partner.

At the same time, as the suburbs grew, Chicago itself prospered as never before under the powerful leadership of Mayor Richard M. Daley, and Roosevelt University was a major beneficiary. The South Loop was the new frontier within the city, a place of dynamic revitalization. Families were moving into brownstones and condominiums in Dearborn Park and Central Station – the mayor among them – just south of the university. Local schools like Jones Academic Magnet High School, with which Roosevelt developed a strong partnership, were restoring faith in public education. More than 40,000 students were pursuing degrees or taking course work at various institutions of higher learning in the South Loop, and student residential halls began to appear throughout the area. Given enrollment growth at the Chicago Campus, the plan to recruit regionally, and the attractiveness of the city, we knew that the Herman Crown Center would not satisfy the needs of our students. We participated with South Loop neighbors DePaul University and Columbia College Chicago in a major residential complex for students called the University Center of Chicago. Currently being developed, it will be eighteen stories high, accommodate 1,720 students, and be located at State Street and Congress Parkway. The University Center of Chicago is owned by the Educational Advancement Fund Inc., a not-for-profit corporation of which Roosevelt is a member, and is financed through a bond issue to be repaid by student fees. University Center will be open for occupancy in 2004 and continue the renaissance of the South Loop. Roosevelt projects it will house 315 of its students in the center, which will supplement the 230 now in the Herman Crown Center. If regional recruitment and the executive MBA for Chinese students continue to attract increasing enrollments, there will be a growing demand for housing and a stronger presence of the university in the South Loop.

2001 To accommodate strong enrollment growth in downtown Chicago, Roosevelt rented five floors of the Gage Building at 18 South Michigan and named the facility the Center for Professional Advancement. The center has 82,000 square feet of space, 34 classrooms, 400 computers, five student lounges, a virtual newsroom for journalism, and multi-media and telecommunications labs. The facility houses the downtown offices of the Evelyn T. Stone University College, Walter E. Heller College of Business Administration, School of Communication and School of Computer Science and Telecommunications.

2000 The Auditorium Theatre was lit up by hundreds of flash bulbs on May 21, 2000, when Oprah Winfrey walked across the stage to deliver Roosevelt University's commencement address and receive an honorary degree. One of the most admired and influential women in the world, Winfrey spoke at Roosevelt because her former personal assistant received an undergraduate degree in business.

Recognizing this rebirth of Chicago, we have expanded our presence through the Center for Professional Advancement at 18 South Michigan Avenue, just four blocks north of the Auditorium Building; it includes the Business College, University College, and the computer science and communication programs of the College of Arts and Sciences – pragmatic, professional programs. Remaining in the Auditorium Building are the Colleges of Arts and Sciences, Performing Arts, and Education as well as the central administration. We moved into the Center for Professional Advancement on December 20, 2000, and offered the first classes in the spring semester of 2001. Roosevelt University has claimed Chicago as its campus, and the university, together with the thriving city, has become a magnet for students from the city, the suburbs, and the nation – and indeed from countries throughout the world. If ever the word renaissance has a literal application to a university and its city, it is embodied by Roosevelt and Chicago.

In the midst of the new Roosevelt University that was emerging so rapidly in the late '90's, a presidential search was launched. I had gone to the chairman of the board, James Mitchell III, early in my third five-year term and indicated to him that I wished to return to the classroom as a professor of American Studies so that I could write several books I could never quite complete so long as I remained president. Jim asked trustee Donald Hunt, former president of Harris Bank, to be chairman of the search committee, and the process went forward. A pamphlet was developed that described the university in eloquent terms; a search committee was assembled and worked diligently; a firm was hired that provided professional support, and a confidential process then proceeded to identify candidates. The attractiveness of the position and the superb finalists who emerged testified as to how far the university had traveled in prestige and importance during the past thirteen years.

> What do I know for sure? Challenges and difficulties are going to come, and they're going to come and they're going to come again. That's what being human is.
>
> OPRAH WINFREY
> ENTERTAINER,
> IN A COMMENCEMENT ADDRESS AT
> ROOSEVELT UNIVERSITY
> 2000

Then the prospect of a merger with National-Louis University emerged, which meant that the candidates who thought they would be leading a university of 7,300 students would be asked to be president of an institution that had 15,000 and had campuses spread across the suburbs, the nation and foreign countries. The candidates themselves could not be made aware of the tentative negotiations, nor could the Roosevelt community, for fear that they would unravel; but once the merger became a real possibility, the presidential search was postponed and I was asked to remain as president for another two years to work out the union of Roosevelt and National-Louis Universities.

Unfortunately, the merger has not been realized, largely because of National-Louis's financial difficulties. But the other projects that my colleagues and I have initiated are still in their formative stages and can now be firmly established within the context of this larger university. The risk management/insurance program is the only one of its kind in a community that is the second largest center for insurance in the nation. The Chicago School of Real Estate now comprises the fourth school within the Walter E. Heller College of Business Administration. Its newly appointed leader – Jon DeVries – occupies the Gerald Fogelson Endowed Professorship in Real Estate, and will help to establish the school of real estate as one of the greatest in the nation; DeVries comes to this position with vast experience, most recently as a Principal in the real estate unit of Arthur Andersen. Three hundred executives from China have studied for the MBAs and there could be created a Center for Chinese and American Commerce and Culture. The Chicago College of the Performing Arts is on the verge of becoming the great conservatory for the city. The Roosevelt Scholars program will have 150 highly selective students in fall 2002.

Throughout the fourteen years of my presidency, the faculty has increased significantly. In 1987 there were 151 full-timers; in 2002, there were 210. Salaries have doubled – from $29,500 to $58,500 –

> True culture begins with the knowledge… of foreign languages.
>
> THOMAS MANN
> AUTHOR,
> IN A TALK AT ROOSEVELT UNIVERSITY
> 1948

and adjusted for inflation, real increases have grown by 31%. In national and state comparisons of faculty salaries, Roosevelt now ranks among the highest in its category of comprehensive universities.

In addition to these programmatic and personnel achievements, several new administrative appointments have been made that will prepare Roosevelt for one of the largest capital campaigns in its history. Led by President Charles R. Middleton and by Judith Kaufman, the recently appointed Vice President of Development, it promises to place Roosevelt on a wholly new plateau of prominence. Kaufman has had an extensive background in fundraising at IIT, the Chicago Historical Society, and other non-profit organizations, and has already strengthened the development office in preparation for the fund drive.

In Schaumburg, an attractive dining center has been established. Soon the entire main building will be completed. Plans for further development of the 30-acre campus are already underway and will be implemented during the next capital campaign. With Schaumburg as the hub, the Albert A. Robin Campus has already developed spokes that radiate to Elgin, Arlington Heights, Streamwood, and other cities; and it will continue to do so.

In Chicago, Roosevelt is a dominant university in the South Loop with the Auditorium Building (430 South Michigan Avenue) facing Buckingham Fountain, the Center for Professional Advancement (18 South Michigan) overlooking Millennium Park, and housing within the University Center of Chicago at State Street and Congress Parkway. Roosevelt was a city college, then a city university – but now it is much more.

On April 2, 2002, after a search that was resumed in the 2001-2002 academic year, the Board of Trustees announced the appointment of a new university president.

Charles R. Middleton comes to Roosevelt University with vast experience as Dean of the College of Arts and Sciences at the University of Colorado at

2002 Board Chairman James J. Mitchell (right) introduced new Roosevelt President Charles Middleton to the Roosevelt community at a reception on April 3. At a press conference earlier in the day, Middleton, vice chancellor for Academic Affairs in the University of Maryland System, said, "In each of my visits to the Roosevelt campuses I have felt the magnetic pull of the community, and I have resonated to the values of the university, both personally and professionally."

2002 Three of the five presidents in Roosevelt University's history visited on the day Charles Middleton was announced as president. From left are Theodore L. Gross, president from 1988 to 2002, Rolf A. Weil, president from 1964 to 1988 and Middleton, who assumed the presidency on July 1, 2002.

Boulder, then Provost and Vice President for Academic Affairs at Bowling Green, and finally as Vice Chancellor for Academic Affairs at the University System of Maryland. His presidency will comprise the fourth chapter in the continuing chronicle of Roosevelt University.

At the turn of this new century, 57 years after it was first conceived, Roosevelt University has been reborn. What began as an experiment in the imagination of Chicago in 1945 now is more than a reality – it is a powerful institution of 7,500 students taught by one faculty in a common curriculum. Although it has grown larger and spread itself geographically, Roosevelt remembers its roots by providing an education for those from all walks of life, from all races and religions and nationalities, who enter the vast middle class, without which there can be no vital democracy or future for America. It is a university true to its core mission of social justice, the reason for its creation and the *raison d'etre* of its future – and now, with a heightened focus on preparing teachers, it can affect schooling profoundly in metropolitan Chicago. Franklin Delano Roosevelt anticipated the purpose of the university named after him when he noted that "The test of our progress is not whether we add more to the abundance of those who have much; it is whether we provide enough to those who have too little." Where better to begin than in the schools?

The spirit of Franklin and Eleanor Roosevelt pervades this university. It is indeed their academic child, anchored by FDR in pragmatism, by Eleanor in idealism. When she said that Roosevelt "was dedicated to the enlightenment of the human spirit," she lit the torch of the university forever. For 57 years it has had this extraordinary history and its future burns brighter and warmer than ever.

Commencement Speakers and Honorary Degree Recipients, June 1946–April 2002

Roosevelt University, Commencement Speakers and Honorary Degree Recipients, June 1946 – April 2002

Date	Speaker
June 10, 1946	Frank W. McCulloch Director, James Mullenbach Industrial Institute
January 27, 1947	Preston Bradley Pastor, The Peoples Church
June 9, 1947	Vera Micheles Dean Research Director, Foreign Policy Association
January, 1948	Herman Finer Professor of Political Science, University of Chicago
June 6, 1948	Oscar Ross Ewing Administrator, Federal Security Agency
January 30, 1949	Bartley C. Crum Publisher, *New York Star*
June 12, 1949	Marshall Field III Owner of Marshall Field's Department Store
August 14, 1949	Robert E. Merriam Alderman, Fifth Ward
January 29, 1950	Jacob J. Weinstein Rabbi, K.A.M. Temple
June 11, 1950	Vijaya Lakshimi Pandit Ambassador, India
January 29, 1951	Walter P. Reuther President, United Automobile Workers, C.I.O. Member, Board of Trustees of Roosevelt College
June 12, 1951	Leo A. Lerner Editor and Publisher, Chicago North Side Newspaper, Chairman of the Board, Roosevelt College
September 9, 1951 (Class Day)	Homer Jack Social Activist
January 28, 1952	Eric L. Kohler Business Consultant, Vice Chairman of the Board, Roosevelt College
June 8, 1952	Guy E. Reed Executive Vice President and Director, Harris Trust & Savings Bank; President, Chicago Association of Commerce and Industry
September 11, 1952 (Class Day)	Dr. Carl Rogers Professor of Psychology, University of Chicago
February 2, 1953	Robert J. Blakely Manager, Central Region Office, The Fund for Adult Education
June 14, 1953	Charles A. Bane Partner, Isham, Lincoln and Beale
September 6, 1953 (Class Day)	Archibald J. Carey, Jr. Alderman of Third Ward and First Alternate Delegate to United Nations
February 1, 1954	Fred K. Hoeler Executive Director, Citizens of Greater Chicago
June 14, 1954	Hugh L. Keenleyside Director General, Technical Assistance Administration, United Nations
September 12, 1954 (Class Day)	Francis S. Chase Chairman, Department of Education, University of Chicago
January 31, 1955	Percy L. Julian President, Julian Laboratories; Member, Board of Trustees of Roosevelt University
June 12, 1955	Henry Steele Commager Professor of History, Columbia University
September 11, 1955 (Class Day)	Charles K. Brightbill Professor of Recreation, University of Illinois
January 30, 1956	Paul A. Wagner President of Film Council of America
June 10, 1956	Lurray D. Lincoln President of Nationwide Insurance
September 9, 1956 (Class Day)	John Ford Golay Dean of Faculties, Roosevelt University
January 28, 1957	Frayn Utley Midwest Director, Institute of International Education
June 10, 1957	James P. Warburg Author
September 15, 1957 (Class Day)	William H. Comog Superintendent, New Trier Township High School
February 3, 1958	Niels Bohr Director, Institute for Theoretical Physics, Copenhagen, Denmark
June 12, 1958	H. Jerry Voorhis Executive Director, Cooperative League of U.S.A.
September 14, 1958 (Class Day)	Leon M. Despres Attorney-at-Law
February 2, 1959	Philip M. Klutznick Member, Board of Trustees, Roosevelt University; Chairman of the Board, American Community Builders; Alternate Delegate to the United Nations; International President of B'nai B'rith
June 16, 1959	Harlan Cleveland Dean, Maxwell Graduate School of Citizenship and Public Affairs, Syracuse University

Date	Speaker
SEPTEMBER 14, 1958 (Class Day)	BLAND BLANSHARD Professor of Philosophy, Yale University
FEBRUARY 1, 1960	EDWIN S. BURDELL President, Cooper Union for the Advancement of Science and the Art
JUNE 13, 1960	W. AVERELL HARRIMAN Secretary of Commerce
SEPTEMBER 12, 1960 (Class Day)	RUSSELL W. BALLARD Director, Hull House Association
JANUARY 31, 1961	JONATHAN PUGH Executive Vice President, Talman Federal Savings and Loan Association
JUNE 12, 1961	LOUIS GOTTSCHALK Professor of Modern History, University of Chicago
SEPTEMBER 17, 1961 (Class Day)	MRS. EUGENIE ANDERSON Former U.S. Ambassador to Denmark
JANUARY 29, 1962	WALTER P. REUTHER President, United Automobile, Aircraft and Agricultural Implement Workers of America
JUNE 10, 1962	HENRY S. REUSS U.S. Congressman, Fifth District, Wisconsin
* JANUARY 28, 1963	WILLIAM O. DOUGLAS Associate Justice, U.S. Supreme Court
JUNE 10, 1963	DAVID D. HENRY President, University of Illinois
FEBRUARY 3, 1964	FRED HARVEY HARRINGTON President, University of Wisconsin, Madison
JUNE 15, 1964	BASIL O'CONNOR President, The National Foundation
FEBRUARY 8, 1965	JOSEPH L. BLOCK Chairman of the Board and Chief Executive Officer, Inland Steel Company
JUNE 21, 1965	ROBERT SARGENT SHRIVER, JR. Director, Peace Corps and Director, Office of Economic Opportunity
JANUARY 31, 1966	MILBURN P. AKERS Executive Director, Independent Illinois Colleges and Universities
JUNE 12, 1966	RALPH W. TYLER Director, Center for Advanced Study in the Behavioral Sciences
FEBRUARY 6, 1967	W. WILLARD WIRTZ Secretary of Labor
JUNE 19, 1967	PHILIP M. HAUSER Professor of Sociology, University of Chicago
FEBRUARY 5, 1968	VIRGIL THOMPSON Musical Composer
JUNE 17, 1968	PHILIP M. KLUTZNICK Commissioner of Housing
FEBRUARY 10, 1969	HOWARD WESLEY JOHNSON President, Massachusetts Institute of Technology
JUNE 16, 1969	WHITNEY M. YOUNG, JR. Executive Director, National Urban League
JANUARY 25, 1970	DANA FARNSWORTH, M.D. Director, University Health Services, Harvard University
JUNE 7, 1970	SOL M. LINOWITZ Lawyer and Diplomat
JANUARY 24, 1971	GEORGE WELLS BEADLE Former President, University of Chicago; Scientist; Nobel Laureate
* JUNE 7, 1971	CORETTA SCOTT KING (MRS. MARTIN LUTHER KING, JR.)
JANUARY 24, 1972	U. THANT Secretary-General of the United Nations (1962-71)
JUNE 5, 1972	ADLAI STEVENSON, III U.S. Senator (Illinois)
JANUARY 22, 1973	EMMETT DEDMON Author, Historian, Journalist, and Scholar
JUNE 4, 1973	JOHN A. ROOSEVELT Member, Board of Trustees of Roosevelt University
JANUARY 21, 1974	CLAYTON KIRKPATRICK Editor, *Chicago Tribune*
JUNE 3, 1974	LLOYD C. ELAM, M.D. President, Meharly Medical College
JANUARY 20, 1975	MILTON FRIEDMAN Economist; Educator
JUNE 2, 1975	FRANK B. FREIDEL Historian
JANUARY 5, 1976	WALTER E. HELLER Economist; Educator
* MAY 10, 1976	ST. CLAIR DRAKE Former Member, Roosevelt University Faculty; Author; Sociologist
JANUARY 5, 1977	CYRIL O. HOULE Educator and Author
MAY 10, 1977	LANDRUM R. BOLLING President, Lilly Endowment; Former President, Earlham College
JANUARY 3, 1978	WILBUR J. COHEN Secretary of Health, Education and Welfare

Roosevelt University, Commencement Speakers and Honorary Degree Recipients, June 1946 – April 2002

Date	Speaker
May 8, 1978	John Hope Franklin, Historian; Professor of History, University of Chicago
January 3, 1979	Norman Alexander Ross, Radio and Television Commentator; Banker
May 14, 1979	James R. Thompson, Governor of Illinois
January 3, 1980	R. Buckminster Fuller, Architect; Professor; Inventor of the Geodesic Dome
May 12, 1980	Hanna Holbom Gray, President, University of Chicago
January 5, 1981	Charles Marshall, President and Chief Executive Officer, Illinois Bell Telephone Company
May 11, 1981	Philip M. Klutznick, Director of Commerce
January 3, 1982	Robert J. Havighurst, Professor Emeritus of Education and Behavioral Sciences, University of Chicago
May 9, 1982	Dan Rather, Broadcast Journalist
January 9, 1983	Cardiss Collins, U.S. Representative, Seventh Congressional, District of Illinois
May 8, 1983	Jerome H. Stone, Chairman, Roosevelt University Board of Trustees
January 8, 1984	Harold Washington, Mayor, City of Chicago
May 6, 1984	James M. Furman, Executive Vice President, John D. and Catherine T. MacArthur Foundation
January 6, 1985	James T. O'Connor, Chairman of the Board, President and CEO, Commonwealth Edison Company
May 19, 1985	Maria W. Piers, Distinguished Service Professor, Erikson Institute
January 12, 1986	Donald P. Jacobs, Dean, J. L. Kellogg Graduate School of Management, Northwestern University
June 1, 1986	Paul Simon, U.S. Senator (Illinois)
January 11, 1987	Harry Mark Petrakis, Novelist
May 31, 1987	Richard Howard Hunt, Sculptor
January 10, 1988	Martin E. Marty, Fairfax M. Cone Distinguished Service Professor, University of Chicago
May 22, 1988	Rolf A. Weil, President, Roosevelt University
January 8, 1989	Alonzo A. Crim, Benjamin E. Olays Professor of Urban Education Leadership, Georgia State University
May 21, 1989	John H. Johnson, Chief Executive Officer, Johnson Publishing Company
	Abraham Lincoln Marovitz, Judge, Illinois Supreme Court
	Ardis Krainik, Director, Lyric Opera of Chicago
January 14, 1990	Sir George Solti, Music Director, Chicago Symphony Orchestra
	Gwendolyn Brooks, Poet Laureate of Illinois
May 20, 1990	Sam Wanamaker, Actor, Director
	Jewel Stradford Lafontant, U.S. Ambassador at Large
January 13, 1991	Ann Landers, Syndicated Advice Columnist
	Warren H. Bacon, Roosevelt University Benefactor
	Richard R. Morrow, Former CEO, Amoco
June 2, 1991	Elie Wiesel, Professor, Author, Humanitarian
January 12, 1992	Danny Newman, Public Relations Counsel, Lyric Opera of Chicago
	Cyrus Colter, Author
	The Honorable Han-Yul Yoo, Congressional Leader, South Korea
May 31, 1992	Alan B. Anixter, Chairman, Roosevelt University Board of Trustees
January 10, 1993	Robert W. Galvin, Chairman of the Executive Committee, Motorola, Inc.

140

Date	Speaker
May 23, 1993	WILLARD L. BOYD President, Field Museum of Natural History
	ALYCE DECOSTA Philanthropist
January 16, 1994	WILLIAM J. BAUER U.S. Appellate Court Justice
	DOROTHY DONEGAN Pianist
May 15, 1994	JOHN F. SANDNER Chairman, Chicago Mercantile Exchange
	DAME KIRI TE KANAWA Concert Artist
January 16, 1995	BILL KURTIS Anchorman, WBBM-TV
May 21, 1995	ARTHUR SCHLESINGER, JR. Award-winning Historian and Author
January 21, 1996	NEWTON MINOW Former Chairman, Federal Communication Commission and the Public Broadcasting Service
January 21, 1996	PATRICK O'MALLEY Chairman Emeritus, Canteen Corporation; Roosevelt University Trustee
May 19, 1996	MARIAN WRIGHT EDELMAN President, Children's Defense Fund
	IRVING HARRIS Chairman, Harris Foundation
	ALBERT A. ROBIN Founder, Robin Companies; Roosevelt University Trustee
January 19, 1997	ADELE SMITH SIMMONS President, John D. and Catherine T. MacArthur Foundation
	KENNETH SMITH President, Chicago Theological Seminary
	DAVID FERGUSON Roosevelt University Chairman of the Board, 1994-1997

Patrick O'Malley

Date	Speaker
May 18, 1997	MANFRED STEINFELD Founder, Shelby Williams Industries
January 18, 1998	BARBARA BOWMAN President, Erikson Institute
May 19, 1998	HENRY FOGEL Chicago Symphony Orchestra
	WILLIAM MASON General Director, Lyric Opera of Chicago
	ZARIN MEHTA Ravinia Festival
January 24, 1999	WILLIAM VANDEN HEUVEL Ambassador, FDR Institute
	ANNA ELEANOR ROOSEVELT University Benefactor
	CHARLES HAMILTON Professor Emeritus, Columbia University; Roosevelt University Alumnus
May 16, 1999	PAUL VALLAS CEO, Chicago Public Schools
January 23, 2000	STANLEY O. IKENBERRY President, American Council on Education
May 21, 2000	OPRAH WINFREY Entertainer
January 21, 2001	LEON LEDERMAN Physicist, Illinois Institute of Technology
May 20, 2001	DANNY K. DAVIS U.S. Congressman (Illinois)
January 13, 2002	SCOTT SIMON Journalist, National Public Radio
	BLANCHE MANNING Appellate Court Judge
April 30, 2002	THEODORE L. GROSS President, Roosevelt University

Manfred Steinfeld

Blanche Manning

Index

Index

Entries in italics indicate depiction in illustrations.

A

Addy, Frederick, 99, *100*, 102, *122*

Adler, Dankmar, 9, 10, 35, 69, 106, 130

African Studies program, founding of, 22

Albert A. Robin Campus (Schaumburg), 43, 86, 92, *98*, 103, 116, *132*; benefits of, 130-131, 136; fundraising for, 119-125, 130; opening of campus, *126-127*

Allen, Harland, 25, *41*; budget disputes with Sparling, 46

Allerson, John, 92, *126*, *133*

Amalgamated Clothing Workers, 28

Ament, Joseph D., *102*

American Assembly of Collegiate Schools of Business (AACSB), 80-81, 99

American Association of University Professors, stand on Lynd case, 61

American Federation of State, County, and Municipal Employees (AFSCME), 28

American National Bank & Trust Co., 130

Amoco, 72, 99, 100, 102, 122

Anixter, Alan, *89*, *91*, *100*, 119, *122*

Anixter Brothers, Inc., 100

Arganbright, Robert, *88*

Arlington Heights Campus. *See* Northwest Campus

Arnold, Wendell, 55

Art Institute of Chicago, 31

Arthur Andersen & Co., 100

Association of Collegiate Business Schools, 103-104

Auditorium Building: *9*, *10*, 27, 35, *50*, *106-107*, 130, *132*; cost of purchase of, 12; cleanup party of, *12*, *13*; creation of by Sullivan and Adler, 9; disrepair of, 54, 87, 125; fundraising for, 124; merger with Roosevelt College, 13, 123; restoration of, 35, 56, 110, 111; *The Untouchables* filmed at, *88*

Auditorium Theatre: *9*, *37*, *38-39*, *40*, *56*, 109; bowling alley in, *10*; deficits of, 82; disrepair of, 87; merger with Roosevelt University, crisis over, 35-37, 40, 43, 111; lawsuit over by ATC, 128-130; performances at, 37, 42; performers at, 12, 110, 111, 128; posters for, *10*; restoration of, 35, 36, 56, 120; as Servicemens' Center, 11-12

Auditorium Theatre Council (ATC), 42, 43, 82; lawsuit against Roosevelt University, 128-130

B

Bachelor of General Studies (BGS) program, 73-74, 104, 124

Baer, Raymond, 69

Barkley, Alben, 51

Barre, Raymond, *78*

Barron, Cynthia, *116*

Baum, Donald, *30*

Belafonte, Harry, 110

Bell, Laird, 34

Bennett, Albert, *104*

Bennett, Marshall, *103*

Bennett, Tony, 110

Bennett, William, 82

Benny, Jack, 17

Benton, Ruth, *121*

Bere, James, *88*

Berkow, Ira, 23

Berkson, Myron, 17

Betty Haag Academy, 110, 111

Bialis, Morris, *63*

Bilandic, Michael, *76*

Black, Conrad, 72, *79*

Black, Hugo L., *123*

Black Metropolis: A Sociology Study of Chicago's Black Community (St. Clair Drake), 22

Black Studies Curriculum, *61*, 63

Bland, Harold, *55*

Board of Trustees, of Roosevelt University, 24-26, 27, *70-71*, 100; backing Weil on tough issues, 56; Gross's recruiting for, 119; as "happy warriors," 26-27; Lerner's resignation from, 40-41

Bohr, Niels, 36, 42

Booth, Sam, 31

Bradley, Preston, 42

Brooks, Gwendolyn, *140*

Brown, Oscar, Jr., 61

Brown, Ron, *96*

Broyles Commission, investigation of Roosevelt University, 29

Buck, Pearl, 26

Budget Committee, of Roosevelt University, 27

Bunche, Ralph, 26

Burnette, Wells, 40

Burrus, Clark, 17

Business College. *See* Walter E. Heller College of Business Administration

C

Carter, Warrick, *133*

Caruso, Enrico, 10, 12

Cassell, Frank, *95*, *125*, *127*, *131*

Center for Chinese and American Commerce and Culture, 135

Center for New Deal Studies, 26, 97

Center for Professional Advancement, 69, 92, 118, 134

Central YMCA College: board of directors of, 4; restrictive covenant of, 3; Sparling's resignation from, 3, 46; resignation of faculty from, 3, 18, 20; Sparling's positions on labor, disagreement over, 28; students of, 4

Champagne, Ronald, *121*, 123, 124

Chicago College of the Performing Arts, 24, 98, 108-110, 111, *112-113*, 135

Chicago Education Alliance, 115

Chicago Musical College (CMC), 23, 35, 57, 108-109, 111

Chicago Public Library, 68

Chicago Public Schools, 75, 76, 82, 89, 115, 116

Chicago School of Real Estate, 103, 135

Chicago State University, 50, 57, 76, 87, 115

Chicago Sun-Times, 62

Chicago Symphony Orchestra, 24, 35, 111

Chicago Tribune, 13, 49

China, recruiting of executives from, 98, 103, 133, 135

Cicarelli, James, *99*, 102

City College of New York (CCNY), 57

City University of New York (CUNY), 97

Clinton, Bill, *96*

Clooney, Rosemary, 110, *113*

College of Arts and Sciences, 75, 93, 96-98, 104, 114, 134

College Bowl tournament, Roosevelt in, *55*

College of Commerce, 77

College of Education, 73-76, 114-116

Columbia College of Chicago, 117, 133, 134

Cosby, Bill, 110, *113*

Creanza, Joseph, *20*, *57*; Auditorium Theatre, attempt to acquire, 36; Chicago Musical College, acquisition of, 35

Cushing, Robert, *121*

D

Daley, Richard J., 46, *68*, 76

Daley, Richard M., 116, 118, *133*

Davignon, Etienne, *79*

DeCosta, Alyce, 69, *72*, *77*, *78*, *79*

"Deep South: A Social Anthropological Study of Caste and Class" (St. Clair Drake & Cayton), 22

DePaul University, 31, 51, 55, 76, 82, 87, 99, 115, 117, 130, 134

Despres, Leon, 28

DeVries, Jon, 135

Dillavou, George, 74

Douglas, William O., 42, 43, *138*

Dunne, Irene, 17

DuPage County Community College, 130

Durnil, J. Michael, *125*

E

Economic Development Commission, 68

Educational Advancement Fund, Inc., 133

Einstein, Albert, 26

Elgin Community College

Ellis, Jerome, *84*

Embree, Edwin, 5, 24, *25;* donations to Roosevelt College, 24, 26
Ethics for Policy Decisions (Leys), 9
Evans, Laura, 108
Evelyn T. Stone University College, 73, 104-105, 134
Eychaner, Fred, 129

F

Fagan, Stuart, 117, *118,* 119, *126*
Feinstein, Michael, 110, *113*
Ferguson, David, *71,* 88, *100, 120-121,* 122, 124, *127*
Field, Marshall, III, *26,* 42, *138;* donations to Roosevelt College, 5, 26, 33
Finding the Center (Graham), 92-94, 116
Fink, Joel, *108, 113*
Fogelson, Gerald, *103*
Ford Foundation, 115
Forest View High School (Arlington Heights campus), 83, *84-85*
Frankel, Norman, 17
Franklin and Eleanor Roosevelt Center for Democratic Values, 26
Franklin and Eleanor Roosevelt Institute (Hyde Park), 26
Franklin, John Hope, *140*
Friedman, Milton, *139*
Fromm, Erich, 80

G

Gage Building. *See* Center for Professional Advancement
Galvin, Robert, *120*
Gandre, James, *112*
Ganz, Rudolph, 23, 24, *26,* 35, *57,* 108
Ganz Hall (Auditorium Building), 24, 40, *81,* 110, *111, 113*
Gear Up program, of Chicago Education Alliance, 115-116
Gertz, Elmer, *63*
G.I. Bill, enrollment at Roosevelt College, 6, 12, 16
Gidwitz, Gerald, *71, 79*
Gilmore, Dulcie *128*
Golay, John, 40

Goldberg, Arthur, *41*
Golden Apple program, 115
Golin, Alvin, 17
Goodman, Bennie, 17
Goran, Morris, *30*
Governors State University, 50
Graham, Bob, 92-93, *94-95,* 116-117
Grant Park (Chicago), *9, 30, 44-45, 49*
Greenberg, Bernard, *30*
Gross, Theodore L., *87, 104,* 119, 131, *137;* achievements of as president, 135-136; and Auditorium Theatre Council lawsuit, 128-130; background of, 88-89, 115; and Board of Trustees, *91,* 119; and Chicago Education Alliance, 115; fundraising of, 94-*95,* 119-124, 136; groundbreaking, *133;* interview of, 88-89; at opening of Schaumburg Campus, *127;* return to teaching of, 134; visits to China and Japan, 114; and Walter E. Heller College of Business Administration, 99

H

Haag, Betty, 110
Hamilton, Charles, 66
Hanauer, Joseph, 17
Hancock, Herbie, 17
Harper Community College, 130
Harriman, W. Averell, 42
Harrington Institute of Design, 117
Harris Bancorp, 100, 134
Heller, Walter E., 69, *78*
Hendry, Mary, *118*
Herman Crown Center, 68-69, 87, 118, 133
Hill and Knowlton, 100, 122
Hiller, David, *122,* 123
Hillman, Arthur, *20,* 31, *54*
Hirsch, Adrienne, *105*
Horne, Marilyn, 110
Houle, Cyril, 74
Huelster, Lowell, 35
Huppi, Rolf, 72, *78*
Humphrey, Hubert, *75*
Hunt, Donald, *101,* 134

I

Ickes, Harold, *26*
Institute for Metropolitan Affairs (IMA), 26, 86, 96, 120
International Ladies' Garment Workers' Union, 28
International Leadership MBA, 103
Iordanou, Constantine, 103, *122,* 123

J

Jacobs, Donald, 17
Jaffe, Aaron, 129
John Pierce Jones Co. Report, on Auditorium Theatre restoration, 37, 40
Johnson, C. Paul, *54,* 99
Jones Academic Magnet High School, *116,* 133
Joseph, John, *125*
Julian, Percy, 8, 24, *25, 41,* 42, *63;* background of, 24-25; postage stamp of, *119*
Julian Laboratories, 25

K

Kamin, Robert J., *71*
Kanawa, Kiri Te, 110
Katten, Melvin, *122*
Kaufman, Edgar J., *77*
Kaufman, Judith, 136
Kaufman Charitable Fund, 77
Kirschner, Don, *54*
Kleinerman, David, 54-55
Klutznick, Philip, *70*
Klutznick, Thomas, *96, 122, 138*
Kohler, Eric, *63*
Kresge Foundation, 123
Krieg, Richard, *96,* 122
Kurtis, Bill, *116*

L

Labor Education Division, of Roosevelt College, 17, 28
Lake County Community College, 130
LaMont, Douglas, 81
Landau, Sara, 8-9
Larson, Al, *127*
Lasch, Christopher, 61
"Laski Lectures" on economics (Harold Laski), 22

Learning for Earning, 75
Lerner, Abba, 13, *20*
Lerner, Leo: 5, *25, 27,* 28, *63;* Auditorium Theatre, opposition to acquisition of, 40-41, 82; background of, 24; donations of, 31, 33; resignation of, 40-43, 46
Lewis, Ramsey, 17, 110
Leys, Wayne L.: 4, 5, *6, 10, 20,* 54; background of, 9; and Broyles Commission, 29; *Ethics for Policy Decisions* (1952), 9; Chicago Musical College, opposition to acquisition of, 35; resignation of, 40
Lind, John, 72
Linneman, Peter, *103*
Logan Square Extension Center, *104*
Lowery, George, *116*
Loyola University of Chicago, 31, 51, 76, 87, 99, 115
Lynd, Staughton, 57-60, *62;* controversy surrounding denial of appointment, 57, 60-63
Lyric Opera (Chicago), 24, 32, 35, 109, 111

M

Makrides, Gregory, 114
Mann, Thomas, 26, 136
Manning, Blanche, *141*
Mansfield Institute for Social Justice, 26
Maremont, Arnold, 37
Martin, Leroy, 17
Marx, Lucy, 73
Mason, William, 17
Matasar, Ann, 81, 99
Mayor's Educational Roundtable, 96
McCormick Tribune Charitable Trust, 123
McCullough, Frank W., 28
McHugh, Ken, *133*
Mednick, Robert, 17, *101*
Mesirow, Norman, *70*
Metropolis Center for the Performing Arts (Arlington Heights), 110
Mid-America Committee, 98, 103, 114

Index

Entries in italics indicate depiction in illustrations.

Middleton, Charles R., 135, *137*
Miller, James, 17
Miller, Yolanda, 108, *112*
Miner, Florence, *120, 124*
Miner, Thomas, 103
Minogue, Rev. John P., *133*
Mitchell, James J., III, *101, 122,* 124, 134, *137*
Mohan-Neill, Sumaria, *99*
Montague, Ashley, 130
Moss, Marvin, *87*
Moss Center, *87*
Motorola, 110, 119, 120, 131
Mulder, Arlene, *127*
Mullins, Rita, *127*
Murray, Phillip, 83
Murrow, Edward R., 66
Music School, of Roosevelt College, 17

N

Natarus, Burton, *133*
National-Louis University, 117, 135
National Organization for Alzheimer's Disease and Related Disorders, 68
North Central Association, accreditation report of, 81, 91, 117
Northeastern Illinois University, 50, 55, 76, 82, 87, 115
North Elementary School (Northwest Campus), 83
Northern Illinois University, 50, 130
North Shore Congregation Israel (Glencoe), 68
Northwest Campus, in Arlington Heights, 83, *84-85,* 122, 123
Northwestern University, 31, 61, 76, 115, 119

O

Oakton Community College, 130
O'Malley, Patrick, *76,* 108, *141*
O'Malley Workshop Theatre, 76, 108, 111, *112-113*
Oracle Corporation, 124
O'Young, Hugh H., *79*

P

Pandit, V. L., 93
Parke, Terry, *127*
Partners in Corporate Education (PIE) program, 105, 108
Peck, Ferdinand W., 106
Pepsi General Bottlers, 120
Percy, Charles, *41*
Perlman, Daniel, 37, 43, *55*
Perlman, Itzhak, 110
Persky, Seymour, 17, 110, *111*
Pettibone, Homer, 34
Pisar, Samuel, *79*
Pitchell, Robert, *47,* background of, 47; diplomatic failure of, 48-49; resignation of, 50
Port, Sidney, *101,* 122
Potenza, Antonia, *118, 126*
Poulsen, Lance, 17

R

Rather, Dan, *140*
Reich, Robert, 96
Reischauer, Edwin O., *79*
Renaissance Campaign, 120-121
Renaissance II Campaign, 124
Reuter, Walter P., 42
Rice, Frederick, 17
Riley, Richard, *115*
Robert Morris College, 117
Robin, Albert A., 83, *85, 101, 122, 127, 131*
Rodriguez, Matthew, 17
Roosevelt, Anna, *82;* annual lecture of, 26
Roosevelt, Eleanor: 24, *27, 46, 82;* dedication of Roosevelt College, *5,* 8; idealism of, 8, 137; on mission of Roosevelt College, 8; raising donor support, 26
Roosevelt, Elliott, 47
Roosevelt, Franklin D., *4;* pragmatism of, 8, 137
Roosevelt, John, 25
Roosevelt College: creation of, 3; equal opportunities for minorities at, 5, 8, 13, 18, 27; first building of (S. Wells St.), 5, *6;* G.I. Bill enrollment at, 6, 12, 16; investigation by Broyles Commission, 29; Labor Education Division, 17, 28; liberal views of faculty of, 29; low tuition costs of, 16; Music School of, 17; non-discriminative policies of, 14; original faculty of, 17; shared governance of, 27; student life at, *14;* Thomas Jefferson College, founded as, 3; trustees of, 24-26
Roosevelt College Opera Workshop, *44*
Roosevelt Scholars, 93, 97, 98
Roosevelt University: accreditation of, 81, 91, 99, 102; African Studies classes at, *30;* biology classes at, *30;* "Centers of Opportunity and/or Excellence" of, 93; competition with other Chicago institutions, 32, 47, 50, 55, 76-77, 87, 99; crisis over Auditorium Theatre, 35-37, 40, 43, 128-130; full-time students, recruitment of, 119; fundraising for, 31-35, 82, *88,* 94-95, 119-124; incorporation of in 1951, 27; international students at, 114; luncheons at, 70; Lynd case, protest over, 61-63; minorities on faculty and staff, 67; National-Louis University, proposed merger with, 135; northwest suburbs, presence in, 83-86, 130-132; older students at, 131-132; physical science classes at, *30;* Pitchell administration, unrest during, 48; Renaissance Campaign of, 120-121; shared governance of, 47; speakers at, 42; sports at, *64-65;* student life at, *31, 44;* student protests at, 56, 58-59, 61-63, 66
Roosevelt University Japan (RUJ), 114
Roosevelt University Orchestra, 111
Rosch, Teryl ann, *115*
Rosenberg, Sam, *97*
Rosenwald, Julius, 5, *25*
Rosenwald Foundation, 5, 26, 33
Rubenstein, Arthur, *57*
Rubloff, Arthur, 86, 96
Ryan, James, *84*

S

Sara Lee, 119
Sawyer, Eugene, *88*
Schaumburg Campus. *See* Albert A. Robin Campus
Schmidt, Helmut, 69, *78*
School of the Art Institute, 117
School of Communication, 134
School of Computer Science and Telecommunications, 120, 124, 134
School of Hospitality and Tourism Management, 122
School of Policy Studies, 96
Schrayer, Max R., *70*
Schub, Earl, 35, 109, 111, *112*
Schweitzer, Albert, 26
Sears, Roebuck, & Co., 25, 119, 131
Servan-Schreiber, Jean-Jacques, *79*
Shannon, Myrtle, *119*
Shelby Williams Industries, 100
Shepard, Robert, *95*
Siegel, Jeffrey, 17
Silverman, Lawrence, 55, 82-83, *84*
Simon, Marion, 110, *116*
Sinatra, Frank, Jr., 110
Singh, Karan, *79*
Sinha, Tarini P., *23*
Smith, Howard K., *41*
Smith, Peter, *127*
Social Action Group, 29
Solti, Sir George, *140*
Spachner, Beatrice: David C. Finley Award received, *56;* fundraising of, 40, 42, 43
Sparling, Edward J.: *2, 10, 18, 27, 29, 46, 81;* Auditorium Building, purchase of, 13; Auditorium Theatre, attempts to merge with university, 35-37, 46, 130; Auditorium Theatre, attempts to restore, 40; background of, 3, 9; and Broyles Commission, 29; Chicago Musical College, acquisition of, 35; dedication of Roosevelt College, *5;* disputes with Harland Allen, 46; fundraising of, 32-34; labor, support of, 28; resignation from

YMCA College, 3; segregation, fight against at Central YMCA College, 3; Thomas Jefferson College, founding of, 3-4; vision for university, 18, 20, 46

Specthrie, Samuel, 77, *80;* as author of accounting textbooks, 80; professorship, *102*

Spencer, Lyle, *49*, 50; Spencer Foundation, 49, 75

St. Clair Drake (John Gibbs St. Clair Drake Jr.): 8, *21*, *30*, 66; African Studies program, founding of at Roosevelt College, 21; background of, 21; *Black Metropolis: A Sociology Study of Chicago's Black Community,* writing of, 22; "Deep South: A Social Anthropological Study of Caste and Class," publishing of, 22; pro-communist accusations against, 29; teaching in Africa, 22, *61*

St. Clair Drake Center for African-American Affairs, 26

Steinfeld, Manfred, 17, *101*, 105, 122, *141*

Steven, Donald, 111

Stone, Jerome, 33, 56, *67*, *68*, *69*, *73*, *79*, *85*, *91*, 119; fundraising efforts of, 68-69, 72-73

Stone Container Corporation, 68, 70

Sullivan, Barry, *88*

Sullivan, Louis, 9, 10, 12, 35, 69, 106, 130

Sullivan Room (Auditorium Building), 110, *111*

T

Tallman, Ronald, 93, *95*

Teitelbaum, Abraham, 13

Terkel, Studs, 61

Thatcher, Margaret, 69, *79*

"This School Bars None" (Landau), 8-9

Thomas Jefferson College, 3-4

Thompson, Vinton, *118*, 119

Through These Portals (Weil), 18, 43, 53

Tippins, Steven, *103*

Torch (Roosevelt student newspaper), 49, *58*

Travis, Dempsey, 17

Tribune Company, 119, 123

Trio, 75

Triton Community College, 130

Truly Disadvantaged, The (Wilson), 86-87

Tucker, Kenneth, 17, *122*, 123

Turner, Edwin, *23*, *44*

Turner, Lorenzo, 8, 22, 66

U

University Center of Chicago, 133-134

University of Chicago, 29, 32, 60, 76, 115, 119

University College. *See* Evelyn T. Stone University College

University of Illinois at Chicago (UIC), 47, 50, 55, 76, 82, 87, 99, 115

Unocal Corporation, 122, 125, 131

Untermyer, Frank, 22, *23*, 48, *61*, 66

Upward Bound program, 75

U.S. Steel, 100, 122

V

van Eck, Bart, *85*, 119

Veterans Upward Bound, 75

W

Walter E. Heller Center, 69

Walter E. Heller College of Business Administration, 69, 81, 98-99, 102, 134, 135; China, recruiting business executives from, 98, 103

Walter E. Heller Lecture Series in International Business and Finance, 69, *78-79*

Warburg, James P., 42

Warwick, Dionne, 110

Washington, Clifton, 75

Washington, Harold, 17, 88

Weil, Rolf A.: *52*, *53*, *63*, *67*, *68*, *69*, *71*, *76*, *85*, *88*, *89*, *137*; achievements of as president, 68, 88; as acting president after Pitchell resignation, 50; background of, 8, 53, 89; fundraising of, 87; inauguration of, 53; leadership qualities of, 54; Lynd case, stand on, 60-63; New Left demands, stand on, 63; on Pitchell administration, 47-48; on political structure of Roosevelt University, 67; Schaumburg Campus, opening, *126-127;* "Statement on Freedom of Expression," 58; *Through These Portals,* 18, 43, 53

Weiner, Lynn J., *97*

Weinstein, Jacob J., 42

Weiss, Bettylou, 129

Wiesel, Elie, *140*

Wieseneck, Robert, 17

William Rainey Harper Community College, 83

Williams, Edward, 17

Wilson, Michael, 69, *79*

Wilson, William Julius, 86

Winebrenner, Howard G., 7

Winfrey, Oprah, *134*, 135

Wirth, Louis, 22

Wirth, Otto, *20*, 48, 75; background of, 54; founding of cultural studies department, 20, 66

Wright, Frank Lloyd, 12

Wright, Raymond, 124

Y

YMCA College. *See* Central YMCA College

Z

Ziegfeld, Florenz, Sr., 23, 35, 108

Zurich American Alumni Hall (Albert A. Robin Campus), 105

Zurich US, 105, 123, 131

EDITORIAL SUPERVISION BY THOMAS R. KAROW

DESIGN AND PRODUCTION BY RAYMOND S. MACHURA

TEXT IS TYPESET IN PLANTIN AND DISPLAY TYPESET IN FRUTIGER

THREE THOUSAND COPIES OF THIS BOOK WERE PRINTED BY MERIDIAN PRINTING

TEXT PAPER IS McCOY VELVET AND THE BOOK IS BOUND IN SIERRA CLOTH